DAY TRIPS in CALIFORNIA Nature

DON'T RUSH ME
I have permission to
dawdle & meander

See page 190

DAY TRIPS in CALIFORNIA Nature

Jayson Loam
Luis Gonzalez
Karen Cunningham

AQUA THERMAL ACCESS

Portola State Park

Grateful acknowledgements to:

Staff members at numerous bookstores and travel agencies for listening to day-trip brainstorms and responding with constructive professional comments; staff members at state parks, state reserves, national forests, national monuments, Indian reservations and private hot spring resorts for their cooperation and encouragement; Marjorie Gersh and Jan Stiles for their superb editorial supervision; the Santa Cruz firms of Lasersmith for print-outs, Bay Photo for film procesing, Dancing Man Imagery for PMT's, John Ryan for computer cover design, Aptos Post for color separation proofs and negatives; all of the subjects who so graciously permitted their photographs to be taken for publication in this book.

Special thanks to Bob Lorentzen for permitting me to adapt material from his book, *The Hiker's Hip Pocket Guide to the Mendocino Coast*. Copies may be purchased by mail from Bored Feet, P.O. 1832, Mendocino, CA 95460. $11.95 plus $2.00 tax and shipping.

Photo Credits:

Luis Gonzalez, 14, 15, 16, 17, 18, 19, 20, 21, 23T 25B, 26, 37L, 37R, 39R, 40, 41, 42L 43R 43BL 44R, 54, 55T, 56L, 57, 58R, 58L, 61R, 62, 63, 64, 65, 66, 67, 68, 69, 70, 71, 72, 73, 74, 75, 76, 79L, 80, 81, 82, 83, 84T, 84R, 88, 89, 90, 91, 92, 93L, 111, 112, 113, 114, 115, 116, 117T, 118, 119T, 119L, 120, 121, 122, 123, 125T, 127L, 132, 133T, 134, 135, 136, 137, 138, 139, 140, 141T; Marjorie Gersh, 9; Phil Wilcox, 84L, 95T, 99L, 99R, 101R; Steve Sutherland, 166, 167T, 169, 170T, 171T, 173, 176, 177T, 178, 180, 181, 185R; Jayson Loam, cover and all others.

Day Trips In Nature: California
Copyright 1991 by Jayson Loam
First Edition 1991
Cartography, design and production by Jayson Loam
ISBN 0-9624830-3-6
Manufactured in the United States of America
Published by AQUA THERMAL ACCESS
       55 Azalea Lane
       Santa Cruz, CA 95060

Table Of Contents

Introduction / 7

Author's Preface / 9

About Your Choices / 13

Directory:
- Grizzly Creek Redwoods State Park / 14
- Jughandle State Reserve / 22
- Russian Gulch State Park / 30
- Vichy Springs / 38
- Harbin Hot Springs / 46
- Sugarloaf Ridge State Park / 54
- Big Bend Hot Springs / 62
- Cottonwood Campground / 70
- Grover Hot Springs / 78
- Buckeye Hot Springs / 86
- Mammoth Mountain Bike Park / 94
- Red's Meadow - Devil's Postpile / 102
- Portola State Park / 110
- Henry Cowell Redwoods State Park / 118
- Forest of Nisene Marks State Park / 126
- Point Lobos State Reserve / 134
- Sand Dollar State Beach / 142
- Montana De Oro State Park / 150
- Cleveland National Forest / 158
- Mt. San Jacinto State Park / 166
- Indian Canyons / 174
- Joshua Tree National Monument / 182

Grover Hot Springs State Park

Introduction

This book is designed to help independent people find and enjoy nonstrenuous, single-day opportunities to experience nature. It is for those individuals who avoid the sweaty burden of a wilderness backpack and who refuse to be herded on and off of tour buses. It is also for those who want their day to include a relaxing soak in a hot pool.

All locations have been chosen for their combination of natural beauty, well-marked trails, and opportunities to interact with the environment. Some locations have a wide variety of available activities suitable for families, seniors and the handicapped, as well as for singles and couples. Even though guided group tours are seasonally available at some locations, these day trips are primarily do-it-yourself excursions. If you find yourself alone on a trail with no buildings or other people in sight, do not panic. Rejoice. You are one hundred percent "in nature," which is one of the goals of this book.

Jughandle State Reserve

Your ability to appreciate nature may have become impaired by the frantic pace and sensory overload of urban living. Spurred on by your hurry-up habits, you may, without thinking, try to set a new track record by zooming through a suggested day-trip program in less than half a day. Please don't.

In order to experience nature with all of your senses, you will need to shut off your go-go compulsion and give yourself permission to dawdle and meander. When you consciously choose to slow down and let in the subtle messages from natural surroundings, you may even get the feeling that you are an integral part of nature. Please do.

Jughandle State Reserve

Author's Foreword: Jayson Loam

The contents of this book grew out of a decade of field research for my two definitive guide books: *Hot Springs and Hot Pools of the Southwest* and *Hot Springs and Hot Pools of the Northwest*. Along the way I noticed that several hot springs were located in or near beautiful, uncrowded, natural surroundings, and I also noticed that a soak in a hot pool was especially enjoyable during, or after, an unhurried walk through those surroundings. Eventually, it occurred to me that some city-dwellers might like to know about such places.

I chose the day-trip format to provide maximum flexibility on the theory that a one-day outing could most easily be incorporated into overall plans for a weekend trip or a week's vacation. Within that format, my mission was to provide all the information, including photographs, that a reader would need to make an informed choice, confirm reservations if needed, and then get to the chosen location.

To meet my criteria, every day trip had to include a soak in a hot pool, so I started with a list of publicly accessible hot springs. Nature did not provide California with enough hot springs in all the right places, so I also chose to include in my list some rent-a-tub establishments where private-space, tap-water hot pools can be rented by the hour. Such hot pools are almost as good as the real thing - and a lot better than nothing.

Using each listed hot pool as a center, I looked within a 30 mile radius for naturally beautiful locations suitable for leisurely, single-day enjoyment. I chose to avoid the famous locations within National Parks and along Interstate Freeways since they attract tour buses and large crowds. Out of this selection process came the final 22 locations reported in this book. Most of them are in State Parks, State Reserves, National Forests, National Monuments, Indian Reservations, and on BLM land. A few are in privately owned resorts.

Wherever possible, I selected locations that offer a wide variety of available day-trip activities, and I have identified those that are suitable for wheelchair use and for families with children. I chose not to describe in detail the provisions for equestrian,

Heartwood Spa

bicycle or backpack use on the theory that such information can best be obtained through organizations that focus on such specialized recreation. I chose to focus on those nonstrenuous single-day activities that encourage people to dawdle and meander, carrying nothing heavier than drinking water, lunch and a camera.

Within each section I chose to provide additional useful data, such as the distance to the nearest airport and the nearest hospital, where to phone or write for information on nearby commercial tourist attractions, and where to write for an official trail map of the area. On the last page of each section, I provide names, addresses, and phone numbers for at least one nearby campground or RV park, and at least one motel or hotel.

Finally, I invite my readers to help me do a better job by informing me of needed corrections and by suggesting improvements in the form and content of future editions. I also welcome suggestions for additional day trip locations. Send your suggestions to:

DAY TRIPS EDITOR
55 Azalea Lane
Santa Cruz, CA 95060

Travertine Hot Springs

Author's Foreword: Luis Gonzalez and Karen Cunningham

Working on this book was a great experience for both of us. We saw many wonderful places and shared the company of some wonderful people. It was fun to observe people inteeracting with nature. Listening to what they had to say about each location we visited added to our own experience.

One thing we heard over and over again was the importance of keeping these places just as they are so that they can be enjoyed time and time again.

While we encourage people to get out and interact with nature, we also encourage the wise and ethical use of nature. As our lives become more fast paced and stress filled, more of us will be seeking out places in nature to interact and add balance to our lives. A little forethought now will go a long way to help insure that places like the ones in this book will be around for us and for those that come after to enjoy.

After having said all that, we hope that you take a little time every now and then to slow the pace and relax. Whether you have several days, or only one, this book can help you get to some unique and wonderful places. As we close our eyes we can still hear the creek gurgling past while we look to the horizon to see the sun's last rays fade, leaving a lavender sky filled with swirling dragonflies overhead and a warm breeze touching our skin.

Nature......you have to experience the feeling.

Grover Hot Springs State Park

DON'T HURRY
You have permission to
saunter & meander

See page 190

Grover Hot Springs State Park

About Your Choices

This book is not an instruction manual, with Steps 1, 2, 3, and 4 to be followed precisely. On the contrary, the information has been chosen and presented in a manner that gives you wide freedom of choice. The following paragraphs are intended to help you make those choices.

Many of the locations described in this book are too large to be fully explored in one day. Therefore, you may choose to engage some nearby overnight accommodations and extend your stay to two or more days.

You may prefer to think of these day trips as itinerary "add-ons." For example, when business or personal travel plans take you to a part of California that has a day trip listed in this book, you may elect to include that day trip in your travel schedule.

Or you may prefer to think of these day trips as last-minute "add-ons," available as spontaneous changes-of-pace when you are in the area. Then you will carry this book with you as an instant resource for that purpose.

You may choose to use the day trips in this book as a starting place to build your travel plans. For example, if you regularly work with a travel agent, you might take this book to the agent, point out a specific day trip, and instruct the agent to build you a weekend "combination getaway" consisting of one day in nature and one day in a resort. Such a plan will give you a leisurely day of individual dawdling and meandering, followed by a more up-tempo day of shopping and mingling.

If you are planning your own vacation via car trailer or RV you can pick from this book the day trip locations you want to include somewhere in your itinerary and then write to the listed visitor information offices for information about nearby commercial tourist attractions. Then you can arrange your very own mix of nature days and tourist days.

After you have initially selected a day-trip location, you will need to obtain additional information by sending for the official map of the area. Also, if you need campground spaces or motel accommodations, you will need to make reservations.

For each location, this book describes several different available activities. To choose among them, you need to consider the described difficulty of the activity, the physical abilities of the individuals in your group, and the current weather conditions. Consult with the ranger or other person in charge when you arrive.

When you visit a forested area, let your intuition help you choose a tree and give it a hug, using your fingertips to explore its texture. While you are there, look closely at the complexities of the bark, and let your nose savor the smell of the tree. Look up through the branches toward the top and listen for the whisper of the wind. If anyone asks you what you are doing, tell them, "I am trying to more fully perceive this one tree so that I will be better able to see the forest."

Wherever you are in nature, choose to do more than just look; be aware of opportunities to interact. Rocks don't shatter when you climb on them, logs don't collapse when you sit on them, and water doesn't wear out when you play in it. Even when you are in motionless repose, with your eyes closed, you can still choose to let your whole body absorb the quiet vibrations of nature. It's good for you.

Finally, we hope that you choose to take care of the beauty you find so that it will bring pleasure to those who come after you. Please remember to, "Take only pictures and leave only footprints." Thank you.

GRIZZLY CREEK REDWOODS STATE PARK

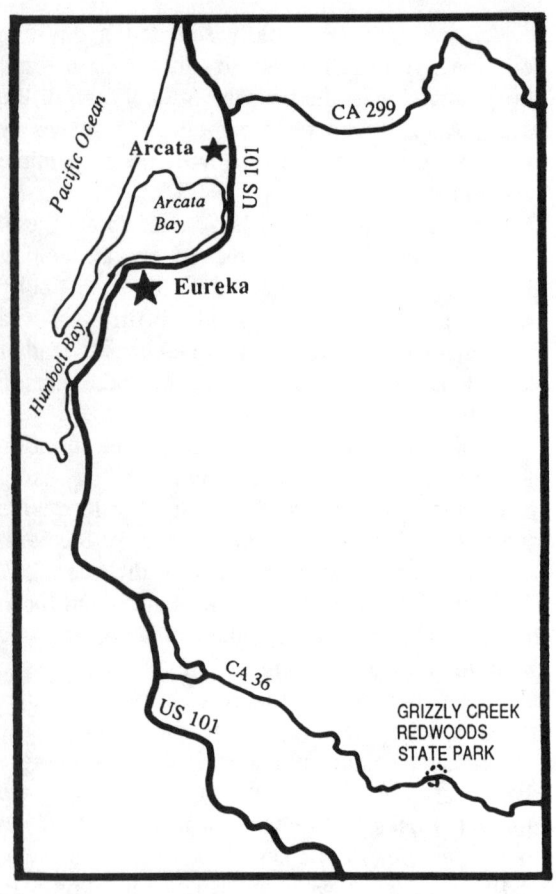

Location Overview

The park covers a 400-acre mostly old-growth redwood forest along Grizzly Creek and the Van Duzen River, 30 miles inland from the Pacific Ocean. It is enjoyable year-round, but foot bridges across the streams are in place only from June until the first winter rains. Elevation: 400 feet.

The available activities are primarily hiking, fishing, canoeing, and swimming. There is a visitor center and a schedule of ranger-led interpretive programs during the summer months. Horses, bicycles and dogs are not permitted on hiking trails.

There are 30 improved campsites, including one handicap site, and six environmental campsites within the park.

It is 20 miles to a motel and 50 miles to private hot tubs for rent by the hour. It is 45 miles to Arcata-McKinleyville Airport, and 20 miles to Redwood Memorial Hospital, (707) 725-3361.

Tourist Attractions

Talk to your travel agent or contact the Fortuna Chamber of Commerce, P.O. Box 797, Fortuna, CA 95540. (707) 725-3959.

Guided nature walks are one of the educational programs available at this park during the summer months.

Trail Maps

This section identifies several of the available activities and does not attempt to provide a detailed map. Therefore, you will need an official map and brochure of Grizzly Creek Redwoods State Park. Send your request with 25 cents to Grizzly Creek Redwoods State Park, 16949 Highway 36, Carlotta, CA 95528, (707) 777-3683.

Expert anglers have a slightly better chance of getting a bite in the deeper portions of this well-stocked stream.

Beginning anglers can enjoy the benefit of parental advice and assistance.

15 GRIZZLY CREEK REDWOODS STATE PARK

When trees are this large it is possible to get to know them from the inside out.

Topography and History

Redwoods are an ancient race. They have survived for more than 20 million years. Their ancestors looked down on the dinosaurs. They once thrived throughout the northern hemisphere, but now are confined to Coastal California. They flourish in a narrow band from the Oregon border to below Monterey, where the climate is moderate year round and heavy winter rains and summer fog nourish these majestic trees.

Coast redwoods, the tallest of trees, can reach more than 360 feet in height, have diameters of more than 22 feet, and live more than 2,000 years. In 1850 there were more than 2 million acres of coast redwood forest in California. At the beginning of the 1990s, only 2.5 percent of that ancient forest remained in a pristine state. These remnants of the ancient forests are contained in redwood parks committed to protecting the few old groves that have survived the ice ages, the uplifting of mountain ranges, subsequent climate changes, and the axe.

Even though Grizzly Creek is near the eastern edge of the redwoods range, it still offers many trees that have reched a height of more than 300 feet. Although these redwoods clearly dominate the park's flora, an entire community of plants exists within the moist, dark climate. Mixed-age "old growth" redwood forests contain more living material than any other forest ecosystem in the world, including tropical rain forests. Redwood sorrel, trillium, glade anemone, calypso orchid, fairy lantern, redwood violet, Douglas iris, wild ginger and sugar scoops are just a few of the plants you will see carpeting the forest floor.

The Nongatl Indians lived here for thousands of years and left hardly a trace of their existence. They were hunters and gatherers of food. The flats near the mouth of Grizzly Creek would have made an excellent campsite for them while they took their share of salmon and steelhead from the fish making their way upstream to spawn. In 1850, while seeking a coastal route to the Trinity gold region, Josiah Gregg and a party of explorers came upon a river and named it the Van Duzen after a member of the group. As farms and ranches were established around the mouth and upper reaches of the Van Duzen the new settlers felt the need to relocate the Indians. In the 1860s army troops out of Fort Humboldt relocated the Nongatl people to a reservation.

Horse-drawn stagecoaches once roared by Grizzly Creek just as logging trucks do today. Highway 36 was part of the main road between Eureka and San Francisco until Highway 101 was improved in 1918. A motor-driven stage to Red Bluff continued using this section of road in the early 1900s. The last stages were different than you might expect - a Cadillac and a Pierce Arrow. Highway 36 was not paved until 1954.

▲ For family enjoyment in nature, consider this combination of clear running stream, sunny beach, and shady forest.

The initial park property was purchased from the Holmes Eureka Lumber Company in 1943 and was officially opened to the public in 1949. In 1966, the area on the south side of the Van Duzen River was added to the park's acreage, preserving additional virgin redwood groves for the public to enjoy. More acreage was added to the park in 1983 with the acquisition of Cheatham Grove from the Save-the-Redwoods League. Located approximately three miles west of the park office, Cheatham Grove offers a spectacular view of pure stands of virgin redwoods. For the camper seeking more solitude than a family campground, six environmental campsites have been established in this area.

▼ The need to care for the forest is most vivid when a child hears about it from a ranger who is an expert on the subject.

▲ River floating may not be as exciting as surfing but it is still a free ride and it can be started at a younger age.

Available Activities

It is possible to explore all 4 1/2 miles of forest trails in a single day. Inquire at the Visitor Center about ranger-led nature walk schedules.

Things to bring: sturdy walking shoes, layered clothing, swimsuit, sunscreen, insect repellant, first aid kit, towel, water, lunch, camera.

All trails have Class 1 surfaces, which means there are no irregularities higher than a standard stair step (nine inches). In addition to fishing and water play in the streams, the following suggested day-trip program will provide examples of several different environments:

Nature Trail Loop through Jameson Grove: 0.7 mile. 50-foot elevation change. Easy self-guided nature trail that includes some stair steps.

Rathert Grove Memorial Trail: 1.2 miles round trip. 100-foot elevation change. Sometimes steep path through dense undergrowth and fallen trees on north-facing slope.

Williams & Graham Grove Hiker's Trail: 1.5 miles round trip. 100 foot elevation change. Sometimes rocky path through tall redwoods, with short, steep sections at each end.

▲ Human beings are dwarfed by the really tall trees found on the Hiker's Trail.

▲ On the Memorial Trail these visitors have decided to sit and recline while deciding where to dawdle and meander.

19 GRIZZLY CREEK REDWOODS STATE PARK

Cheatham Grove Trail: 1.0 mile. 20 foot elevation change. Very quiet level path through moist, dark redwood grove near Van Duzen River.

 Cheatham Grove is so magically beautiful that it was used to shoot the redwood forest scenes in the famous motion picture, *Return of the Jedi*.

▲ This lush greenery at the Finnish Country Sauna & Tubs is an appropriate part of a day trip in nature.

Soak and Sleep

Within the park there are 30 improved campsites, including one handicap site, and six environmental campsites. Reservations are recommended except during winter months; phone MISTIX, (800) 444-PARK from within California; (619) 452-1950 from outside California.

Fortuna Motor Lodge: (707) 725-6993.
275 12th Street, Fortuna, CA 95540. Offers 25 units.

Finnish Country Sauna & Tubs: (707) 822-2228.
5th and J Street, Arcata, CA 95521. A charming, European-style pond surrounded by grass-roofed Finnish sauna cabins, outdoor hot tubs, and a cafe.

▲ It may not be geothermal mineral water, but the pool is outdoors, under the trees, and the temperature is mellow.

JUGHANDLE STATE RESERVE

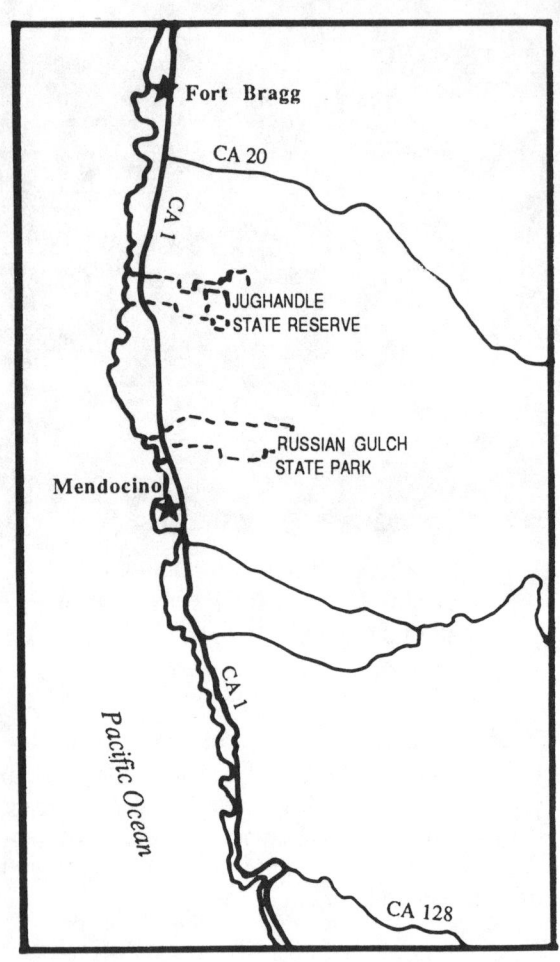

Location Overview

This 800-acre reserve contains the educational Ecological Staircase Trail, which leads through five wave-cut terraces that have uplifted from the sea over hundreds of thousands of years. Family recreation is ideal on the 20-acre beach protected from cold winds by the Jughandle Bay headlands. Elevation: Sea level to 500 feet.

Available activities include hiking, beach play and water play in a fresh water stream and in the ocean waves.

Horses, bicycles and dogs are not permitted on the trails.

The reserve does not include a campground, and overnight parking is prohibited. There is a state park campground within five miles. It is eight miles to motels and to private space hot tubs in Mendocino. It is five miles to Mendocino County Airport and 10 miles to Mendocino Coast District Hospital, (707) 964-1315.

Tourist Attractions

Talk to your travel agent or contact the Coastal Visitor Center, 991 Main St. Mendocino, CA 95460. (707) 937-5804.

▲ This family photo will include a sunlit fern in the pygmy forest on the pygmy forest on the Ecological Staircase Nature Trail.

Trail Maps

This section does not attempt to provide a detailed trail map. Therefore, you will need a Staircase Trail Guide (including official map) of Jughandle State Reserve, and we recommend that you obtain it ahead of time by mail. Send your request with 50 cents to Jughandle State Reserve, P.O. Box 440, Mendocino, CA 95460, (707) 937-5804.

▲ A completely different part of the Reserve is this large beach which has accumulated inside Jughandle Cove.

Topography and History

For a half-million years or more, this part of the Mendocino coast has been rising, jolted upward in response to tremendous forces that have been building the Coast Range. The sea, which rose as a warming climate melted glaciers, cut into the emerging land to create bluffs and beaches that grew larger as sand and gravel were washed down onto them. Then renewed tectonic activity lifted the beaches to form seaside terraces.

The result of this interaction of climate and geology is five wave-cut terraces, each about a hundred feet higher and a hundred thousand years older than the next. The youngest terrace, at the beginning of the Ecological Staircase Trail, emerged from the sea around one hundred thousand years ago; the highest terrace is over five hundred thousand years old. Plants and soils change from terrace to terrace, with redwood and pygmy forests on the higher levels.

In the 1870s, a rail line was constructed along Jughandle Creek to serve the Caspar Lumber Company mill. In the 1880s, the company purchased more timberland to the north and built a trestle over Jughandle Creek canyon. It rose 146 feet high, was 1,000 feet long and carried many huge loads of timber before folding like an accordian in the 1906 earthquake. As late as 1961 there was still some commercial logging of second-growth redwoods. During the 1970s, the State of California purchased several parcels of land from individuals and corporations to create Jughandle State Reserve, which was opened in 1978.

Bowl-shaped Jughandle Cove, typical of the coves along the north coast, has been formed by the shifting of the creek. Before 1976, the creek flowed into the ocean along its north side; now it is widening the cove on the south. The creek is carrying grains of sand from the ancient beaches of the upper terraces to help create a very large beach within the cove. The end result is an excellent location for family recreation.

The west end of the beach is washed by the ocean, getting its share of seaweed and breaking waves. Along the north side, headland cliffs protect sunny stretches of white sand from cold ocean winds. Jughandle Creek runs along the south side of the beach in the form of a long, shallow, sandy-bottom fresh-water pond, ideal for air mattress and inner tube floating.

It is a short hike from the parking lot to a steep little path leading down toward the beach. However, beac-goers must then wade across Jughandle Creek to reach the big pile of dry white sand. This process can become quite an adventure, especially for families carrying lots of beach gear, and not wearing the right shoes for wading.

Available Activities

Hiking the Ecological Staircase Trail at a leisurely pace will require three to four hours. This trail surface is Class 1, which means that there are no irregularities higher than a standard stair step (nine inches). However, there are some actual stair steps to be climbed and some steep sections of trail.

We suggest that the remainder of the day be devoted to exploring possibilities for fun and relaxation on the great white beach.

Things to bring: sturdy walking shoes, sandals for wading and beach wear, layered clothing, swimsuit, sunscreen, insect repellant, first aid kit, towel, water, lunch, camera, beach chairs and inflatable floats.

Ecological Staircase Self-Guided Nature Trail: 5 1/2 miles round trip. 500 foot elevation change. Use the official brochure to get the most out of this vivid demonstration of nature in action.

Jughandle Cove Beach: 1/2 mile round trip. 50 foot elevation change. The trail surface is Class 1 except for a steep and irregular section just above the place where it is necessary to wade across the creek.

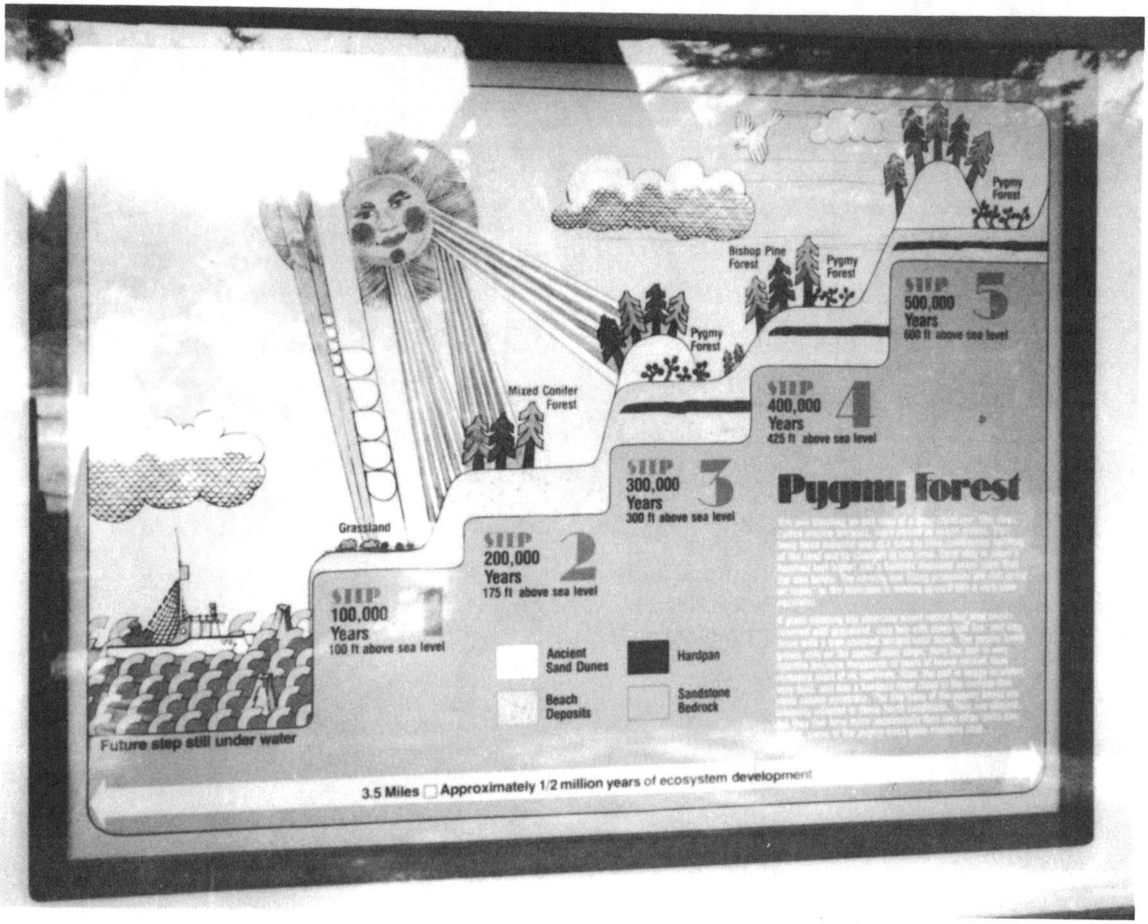

▲ This diagram, mounted at the trailhead, explains how 500,000 years of ecosystem development created the terraces.

▼ Stair steps with handrails have been constructed to assist visitor movement between the various terraces.

25. JUGHANDLE STATE RESERVE

▲ To dawdle and meander one must lean, whenever possible, on bridge railings. This Staircase Trail one will do nicely.

▲ Becoming acquainted with the forest includes seeing and touching new and interesting objects such as pine cones.

▲ Becoming really acquainted with the forest includes tasting that pine cone.

▲▼ There is no bridge over Jughandle Creek at the beach, so visitors have the fun of removing their shoes and wading across in a primitive safari line.

▲ The fast-moving fresh-water crayfish are fun to chase but impossible to catch.

▲
◆ A wind-protected beach is a giant playground for children, especially when
▼ it includes weird forms of seaweed.

DON'T HURRY
You have permission to

dawdle & meander

See page 190

▲ This is Jughandle Beach, the Hwy 1 bridge, and the terraces as seen from the bluff portion of the nature trail.

Soak and Sleep

This reserve does not contain a campground, and overnight parking is prohibited.

Russian Gulch State Park: Located two miles north of Mendocino on the west side of Hwy #1. Offers 30 family campsites with hot showers and flush toilets. Reservations are recommended except in winter; phone MISTIX, (800) 444 PARK from with in California; (619) 452-1950 from outside California.

Mendocino Hotel and Garden Suites: (707) 548-0513.
45080 Main Street, Mendocino, CA 95460. Offering 51 units, garden cafe, balconies, fireplaces.

Caspar Springs: (707) 964-1111.
45310 Pacifica Drive, Caspar, CA 95420. Three outdoor private spaces, each with hot tub, sauna, and shower, available for rent by the hour.

▲ After a full day of climbing the terraces and combing the beach you might want to relax in this outdoor hot tub.

29 JUGHANDLE STATE RESERVE

RUSSIAN GULCH STATE PARK

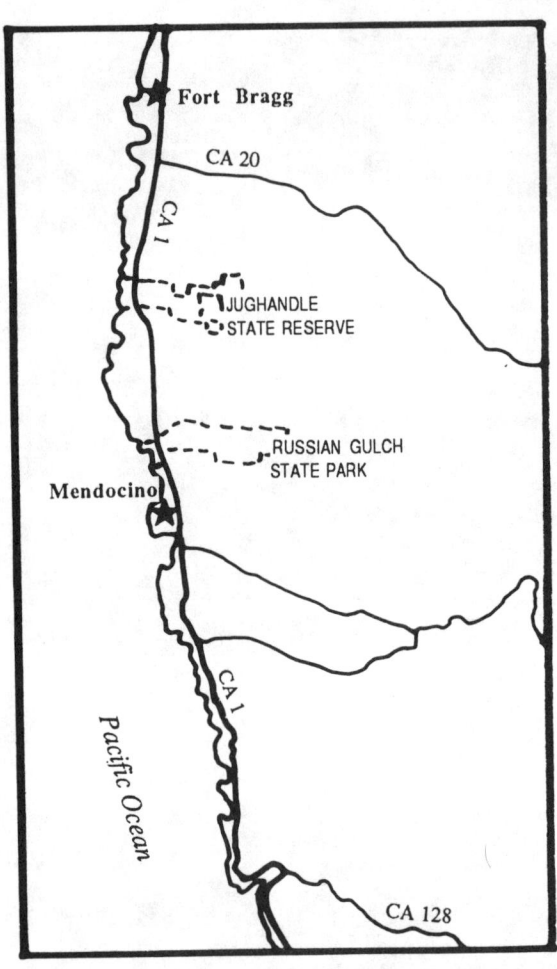

Tourist Attractions

Talk to your travel agent or contact the Coastal Visitor Information Center, 991 Main Street, Mendocino, CA 95460, (707) 937-5804.

Location Overview

This park derives its name from the fact that Russian fur trading ships anchored in the small bay at the mouth of the gulch. The 1,250 acre property occupies the headlands around the bay and extends four miles inland, including lush greenery on both sides of the creek that carved the gulch. It is enjoyable year-round, except when raining. Elevation: sea level to 500 feet.

The available activities include hiking, ocean fishing, and water play in the stream and on the small beach. There is no visitor center, but some ranger-led hikes are conducted during the summer. Horses and bicycles are permitted only on a few designated trails.

There are 30 improved campsites within the park. It is two miles to motels and to hot tubs for rent by the hour, nine miles to Mendocino County Airport, and eight miles to Mendocino Coast District Hospital, (707) 964-1315.

▲ When hikers on the Waterfall Trail reach this view point they get a fine first view of the fall's dramatic tracery.

▲ At the opposite end of the park, on the ocean headlands, visitors by the safety fence are dwarfed by this huge blowhole.

Trail Maps

This section identifies only some of the available activities and does not attempt to provide a detailed trail map. Therefore, you will need an official map of Russian Gulch State Park, which is contained in *North Wind*, the Mendocino Coastal District Guide. We recommend that you obtain it ahead of time by mail. Send or phone your request to Department of Parks and Recreation, P.O. Box 440, Mendocino, CA 95460, (707) 937-5804.

▲ The flat plateau above the cliffs was formed as a sedimentary sea bottom and then lifted by immense geologic forces.

Topography and History

The Mendocino coast was born about 40 million years ago, the result of the collision of two giant pieces of the earth's crust (tectonic plates). As the North American plate moved substantially westward, it collided with and overrode the Pacific plate. The Coast Ranges were built by the sedimentary material scraped from the Pacific plate in this process. Though the collision became more gentle over the ensuing eons, the plates continue to collide today.

Over the last million years, a series of five to seven marine terraces have been successively uplifted, each one serving its time as the sea coast before being pushed farther above sea level. Rain water coursing toward the ocean carved dozens of gullies, which grew into moist and shady gulches and canyons as the streams eroded ever-deeper notches into the uplifted terraces. The San Andreas Fault now forms the dividing line between the two tectonic plates. The Pacific plate to the west of the fault began to move northward about 25 million years ago.

▲ Sure-footed anglers have ventured onto this tiny ledge to try their luck at surf casting into the sea 50 feet below.

Two distinct plant groups mingle on the Mendocino coast. Plants of a cooler, wetter climate migrated from the north. These include redwood, fir, spruce and tanoak. Representatives of the drier, warmer climate of the south include madrone, manzanita, bay laurel, Bishop pine and ceanothus.

Archaeological evidence taken from shell mounds shows that Native Americans lived along the coast for at least 4,000 years before the settlers came. The first Spanish galleon is believed to have sailed along the Mendocino coast about 1545. The Russians also had their time along the coast, establishing Fort Ross in 1812. The name Russian Gulch originated because the Native Americans told of seeing white men there with a large ship in the late eighteenth century. Having exhausted the fur trade by 1841, the Russians abandoned the coast.

With the coming of the California gold rush beginning in 1848, Americans began to explore the North Coast, seeking timber and other resources to supply California's booming growth. By 1900 there were more than three dozen towns on the Mendocino coast, all connected to the timber trade. The tiny mill towns and ports came and went, but by 1940 fifty sawmills were scattered along the coast. Improved roads and modernization brought centralization; by 1960, only three mills and a dozen towns remained.

The climate of the Mendocino coast is cool, but mild enough for year-round hiking if you are prepared for varying conditions. Keep in mind the following about the seasons in this area:

November to March are the rainy months, time to bring raincoats and rubber boots. Still, there are often fine sunny days between storms.

April and May are often windy, with occasional rainstorms. The wind may be gentle or fierce and unrelenting. The landscape is at its most lush and beautiful. Bring layered clothing and hats.

June, July and August bring sunny summer days alternating with thick fog, which may burn off inland but sometimes clings all day along the beaches.

September and October are a beautiful time with many fogless days. Though there may be an occasional rainstorm, most of the days are calm and warm. The land is dry, the hills golden, and the sunsets often spectacular.

▲ The Hwy 1 bridge over Russian Gulch is part of the view from this picnic area.

Available Activities

Your day-trip plans should be adjusted to fit current weather conditions and the physical abilities of the individuals in your group. Discuss them with a ranger when you arrive in case one or more of the suggested activities should be changed for your comfort and convenience.

Things to bring: sturdy walking shoes, layered clothing, swimsuit, sunscreen, insect repellant, first aid kit, towel, water, lunch, camera.

Trail surfaces are classified as follows:

Class 1. Generally smooth with no irregularities higher than a standard stair step (nine inches).

Class 2. Some irregularities higher than one standard stair step but none higher than two stair steps (18 inches).

Class 3. Some irregularities higher than 18 inches.

The total trail system of this location is too large to be fully explored in one day. The following suggested day trip program will provide examples of several different environments:

Headlands Trail Loop: 0.7 mile. Minor elevation change. Class 1 trail surface. The blowhole and natural bridges along this trail illustrate how the ocean is gradually wearing away the headland cliffs.

South Trail: 0.9 mile. 300-foot elevation change. Class 1 trail surface. This path leads through lush greenery and a large fir forest on the ledge above the canyon. There are some steep sections leading up out of the canyon.

Waterfall Trail Loop: 6.2 miles. 500-foot elevation change. Class 1 surface. This entire hike goes through sweeping vistas of tall trees and lush vegetation reaching up high canyon walls. The first 1.6 miles are on a partially paved road, rising gradually uphill along the edge of the creek and suitable for street bikes as well as for hiking. The next 0.9 mile section is a winding path with some stair steps, leading to a gorgeous waterfall. The top of the loop (2.1 miles) includes many stair steps and some steep sections to reach the stream above the waterfall and then return downstream along another branch of the creek.

▲ For the convenience of bicycle riders a secure metal bike rack is provided where this wide trail narrows to a windy path.

▲ This enterprising tree sprouted on top of a stump and then had to grow roots down the side of the stump to survive.

▲ A thoughtful chainsaw operator did more than cut through this fallen tree; he also carved a handy seat for hikers.

▲ In this short steep section of the path rustic steps have been constructed to prevent the trail being washed out.

▲ The top of this old stump has accumulated enough debris to nourish a small forest garden, including trees.

▲ This picnic spot by the waterfall has the look and the sound of a tropical rain forest but air is always cool.

▲ The ability to dawdle and meander includes stopping for a social chat with hikers going the other way on this path.

A small number of well-shaded campsites line the creek bank in this state park.

Customers at Sweetwater Gardens can rent a private-space hot tub large enough for two, or they can choose to share the huge communal hot tub which might attract a crowd of a dozen or more.

Soak and Sleep

The campground in this park has hot showers, flush toilets and 30 improved campsites. Reservations are recommended except during winter months. Phone MISTIX, (800) 444-PARK from with in California; (619) 452-1950 from outside California.

Mendocino Hotel and Garden Suites: (707) 548-0513.
45080 Main Street, Mendocino, CA 95460. Offering 51 units, garden cafe, balconies, fireplaces.

Sweetwater Gardens: (707) 937-4140.
955 Ukiah Street, Mendocino, CA 95460. Large communal hot pool with sauna and two private-space hot pools for rent by the hour. Some overnight accommodations with hot pool access are also available.

VICHY SPRINGS

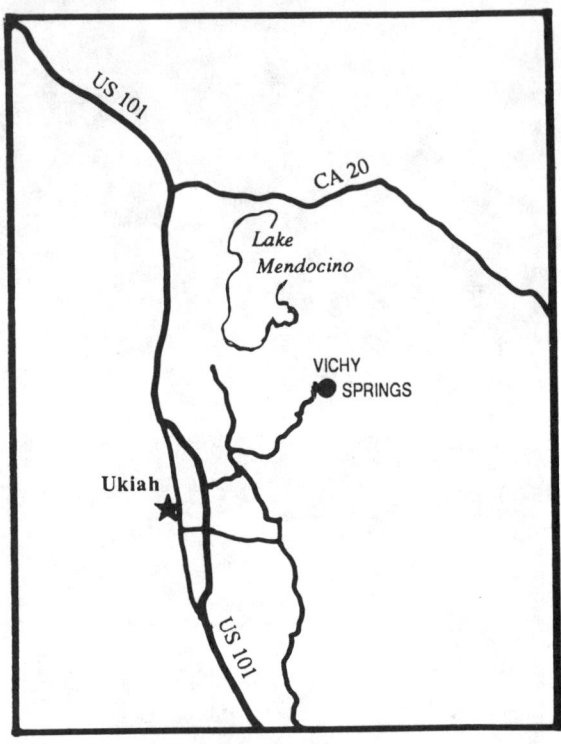

Location Overview

This charming, privately owned resort and ranch covers 700 acres on the west slope of the Mayacamas mountains. It has its own mineral-water spring and flowing stream with waterfall. The best weather is during spring summer and fall. Elevation: 800 to 3,100 feet.

The available activities are primarily hiking, bicycling, mineral-pool soaking, swimming, massage and hand and foot reflexology. The facilities are available to day-use customers as well as to registered guests.

Rooms and cabins in a parklike setting are available on the premises, as is overnight parking for self-contained RVs. It is 12 miles to tent camping sites at Lake Mendocino; five miles to the Ukiah Municipal Airport, and four miles to Ukiah Valley Medical Center, (707) 462-3111.

Tourist Attractions

Talk to your travel agent or contact the Ukiah Chamber of Commerce, 495E E. Perkins Street, Ukiah, CA 95482, (707) 462-4705.

This plaque identifies Vichy Springs as being a California historical landmark.

▲ A Japanese-style bridge spans Little Grizzly Creek near the new soaking pool.

▲ A mile upstream the creek has formed a shallow rock pool at the waterfall.

Trail Maps

There are no "official" maintained trails, and therefore no trail map. A primitive path follows the streambed to a waterfall. Eight miles of ranch roads are designated for mountain bicycling and a ranch road map is available. To obtain a resort brochure with information on accommodations and rates, write to Vichy Springs Resort, 2605 Vichy Springs Road, Ukiah, CA 95482, (707) 462-9515.

▲▼ Some portions of the stream run through volcanic bedrock while others run through banks of sand and gravel.

Topography and History

The rolling hills with woods, meadows and streams, are sometimes chilled by winter fog and baked by summer sun, but the area is delightful year-round. During late summer months the surface stream may slow to a trickle.

The flow of the mineral springs from miles deep in the earth is not affected by weather cycles. Named after the world-famous springs first discovered in France by Julius Caesar, the virtually identical water of Vichy Springs surges forth in abundance just as it has for thousands of years. First used by Native Americans, the bubbling waters have since become known as "Champagne Baths." The property also includes an old cinnabar mine that used to produce commercial quantities of quicksilver, a resource often found in geothermally active ground formations.

Founded in 1854, Vichy Springs is the oldest continuously operating spa in California and is now a California Historical Landmark. The idyllic parklike setting was a favorite retreat of writers Mark Twain, Robert Louis Stevenson and Jack London, as well as Presidents Ullyses S. Grant, Benjamin Harrison and Teddy Roosevelt.

The resort has been restored and renovated as a bed and breakfast inn to tastefully combine its natural and historic charm with modern comfort and convenience. Twelve individually decorated rooms with private baths date from the 1860s, while two one-bedroom cottages built in 1854 now have fully equipped kitchens. All accommodations have their own heating and air conditioning.

▲ Overnight accommodations and picnic tables are scattered over several acres of beautiful tree-shaded lawns.

◄ The bank behind the soaking pool is composed of a travertine onyx formation built up over thousands of years by the mineral spring which is still flowing.

▲
▼ The Little Grizzly Creek environment includes both sunny broad channels and narrow channels where trees meet.

Available Activities

Practically anything you choose to do at this secluded, self-contained resort is quietly "in Nature." The overnight accommodations open onto flowerbeds and a parklike, tree-shaded central lawn, and the mineral-water soaking pools are bordered by cliffs of ancient travertine deposits.

Things to bring: sneakers that can get wet and still be comfortable, layered clothing, swimsuit, sunscreen, insect repellant, first aid kit, towel, water bottle, lunch, camera.

Little Grizzly Creek to the waterfall: 2.4 miles round trip. Minor elevation gain. Although generally smooth, the primitive path does require some boulder hopping, log walking, and wading through the creekbed.

"Champagne Bath" soaking: unlimited use of a dozen historic indoor and outdoor cement tubs just the right size for two persons. Fill the tub of your choice with fresh, bubbly mineral water piped directly from the nearby spring. Also, there is unlimited use of a large, outdoor mineral-water hydropool that is maintained at 104 degrees, and of a chlorine-free swimming pool.

Massage and Hand and Foot Reflexology: Available by appointment (extra charge) in the building next to the hydropools. Couples may arrange for simultaneous massages on adjoining tables.

▲ A muddy torrent during winter rains, the waterfall becomes a joyfully-splashing sparkling clear necklace in the spring.

▲ By mid-summer the waterfall slows to a trickle which complements a picnic lunch by murmuring gently in the background.

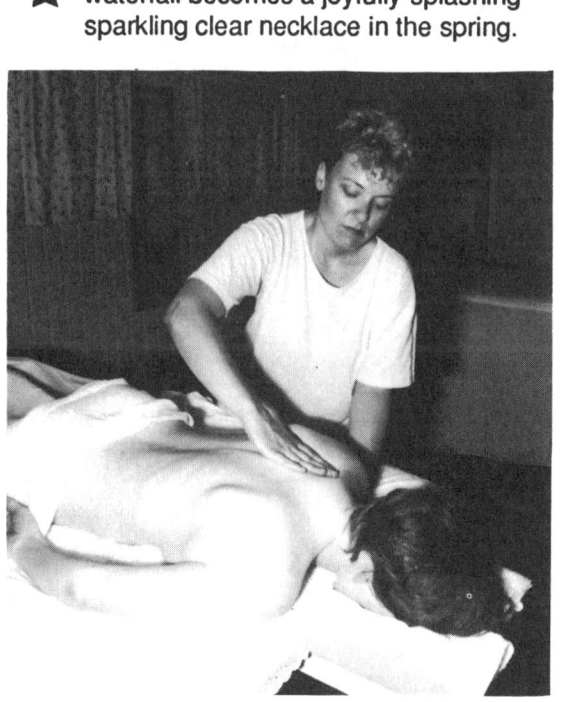

▲ Intriguing black salamanders have their homes in Little Grizzly Creek pools.

◄ Massage and reflexology are available in a building next to the soaking pools.

Soak and Sleep

The resort is a bed and breakfast inn offering rooms and cabins. Overnight parking is available for self-contained RVs. Mineral-water soaking pools, massage and hand and foot reflexology are also available on the premises. No tent camping is permitted.

Lake Mendocino Campgrounds: (707) 462-7581. 12 miles from Vichy Springs. Four campgrounds around the lake are operated by the Corps of Engineers. Family sites are first-come, first-served.

Discovery Inn: (707) 462-8873.
1340 N. State Street, Ukiah, CA 95482. Offers 158 rooms, swimming pool, and hydropool.

▲ The masseuse will tell the customer when it is time to walk the few feet from the soaking pool to the massage table.

► The crystal-clear swimming pool is located at the edge of the main lawn.

▲ These outdoor concrete soaking tubs date back to the turn of the century. There are also some similar indoor tubs.

▼ Overnight accommodations combine informal historical buildings with modern plumbing and tasteful decor.

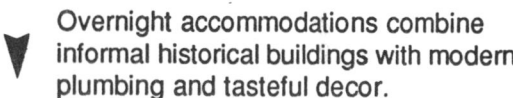

HARBIN HOT SPRINGS

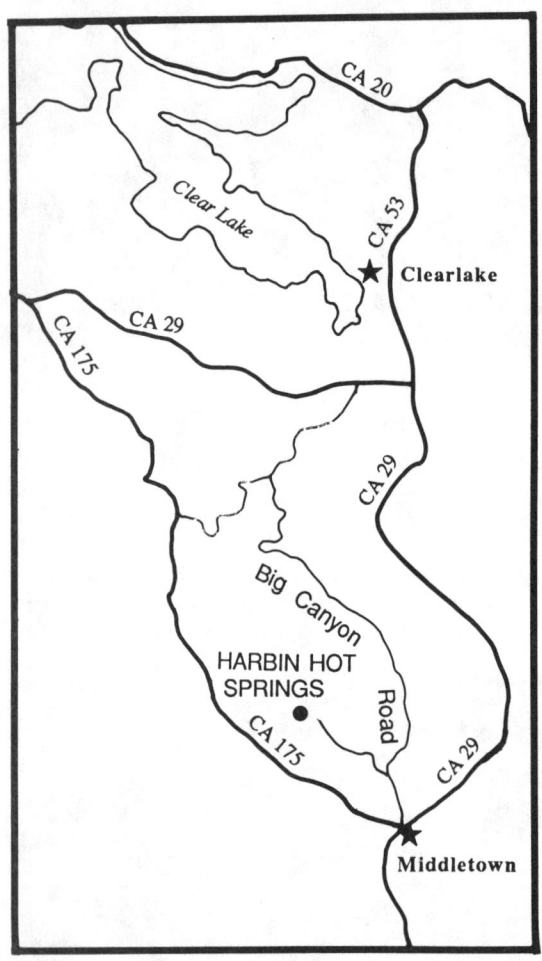

Trail Maps

This section does not attempt to provide a detailed trail map. Therefore, you will need an official trail map of Harbin Hot Springs and vicinity, and we recommend that you obtain it ahead of time by mail. Send your request to Harbin Hot Springs, P.O. Box 82, Middletown, CA 95461, (707) 987-2477. Also, we recommend that you request information about the philosophy of Harbin Hot Springs and the New Age residential community that operates the facility.

Location Overview

This 1,100-acre conference and retreat center in Lake County presents a truly unique combination of environment, facilities, and policies. Nestled in a quiet valley, it offers hiking trails, multiple mineral-water pools, streamside camping sites, and rooms in several buildings, all with a policy of clothing optional. Clothing is required in the dining hall. Harbin is open all year, and the pools are open 24 hours a day. Elevation: 1,700 feet.

The available activities are primarily hiking, soaking and sunbathing. Solstice and Full Moon ceremonies are open to everyone. No pets are allowed.

All overnight accommodations, except RV hookups, are available on the premises. It is 50 miles to Santa Rosa airport and 20 miles to Redbud Hospital, (707) 999-6486.

Tourist Attractions

Talk to your travel agent or contact the Clearlake Chamber of Commerce, P.O. Box 629, Clearlake, CA 95422, (707) 994-3600.

▲ Resort buildings dating back to the turn of the century have been renovated and expanded by the new ownership group.

▼ Harbin is one of the few commercial hot-spring resorts where clothing is optional, including sun deck and pools.

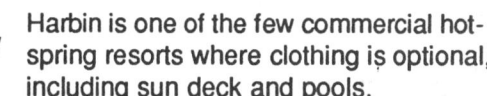

47 HARBIN HOT SPRINGS

▲
▼ Across a road and stream from the main buildings, Harbin Springs has built this conference center for New Age groups who want a natural environment.

Topography and History

It took thousands of years of volcanic eruptions to build up the mountains in this Lake County area - and thousands of years of snow and rain to carve them into the present jumble of peaks, valleys and lakes. More than a dozen hot springs as well as the vast geothermal power plant at the The Geysers demonstrate that the molten magma of inner earth is still very close to the surface.

The Pacific Ocean is only 40 miles away, but the moderating effect of ocean breezes seldom reaches over the intervening series of mountains, some of them over 4,000 feet high. Some upper-level snow is expected in the winter, and daytime summer temperatures are often in the 90s, dropping into the 60s at night. Storm fronts sweep in from the ocean from late fall through early spring, but even in winter there are usually a few sunny days between the downpours. Most of the large stands of cedar, fir and pine were logged off by the turn of the century, leaving primarily oak, madrone, alder and manzanita.

Clothing is required in the dining hall and on the adjoining deck which overlooks the community gardens.

The mineral springs and their curative powers were well known to the local Indian tribes long before white settlers arrived and imposed their private property ownership laws. Around 1860, James Harbin became the second owner of the springs which now bear his name, and sold it ten years later. By 1881, a subsequent owner, Richard Williams, had built a substantial resort with a hotel, bar, dining room, bathhouse, numerous cottages and a croquet court. The Harbin Springs stage connected with all trains in Calistoga, and it took only nine hours to make the trip from San Francisco.

After the turn of the century and the growth of modern medicine public belief in the curative powers of mineral water declined, and so did the patronage at hot-spring resorts. Harbin, along with several other Lake County geothermal resorts, entered the downward side of the commercial hot spring cycle, suffering closure and ownership changes. It was purchased in 1972 by one of the founders of the community now known as Heart Consciousness Church, and reconstruction has been slow but steady ever since. In addition to renovating the old existing buildings, the new ownership has built an extensive conference center complex, which is very popular with all types of New Age groups. Brochures describing the goals and the facilities of the community are available on request.

The conference center has its own pool, which is used primarily on weekends, so is kept covered during the week.

Available Activities

Your day-trip plans should be adjusted to fit current weather conditions and the physical abilities of the individuals in your group. Discuss your plans with an attendant when you arrive in case one or more of the suggested activities should be changed for your comfort and convenience.

Things to bring: sturdy walking shoes, layered clothing, sunscreen, insect repellant, first aid kit, towel, water bottle.

Trail surfaces and grades differ widely, and clothing is optional only on those trails that are not visible from a public road. Discuss the condition and clothing policy of each trail before setting out. The following suggested day-trip program includes only trails where clothing is optional and which have a Class 1 surface:

▲ As should be expected, some portions of the Spiritual Path are steep and rocky.

▲ Foliage is so thick that it is difficult to see all of the pools from the path.

▲ A favorite spot along the Spiritual Path is this quiet resting place on a gentle slope shaded with lush green trees.

◄ A few yards from the pool area volunteers have built this shady grotto, complete with vines and a waterfall.

Spiritual Path Loop: 0.9 mile. 50-foot elevation change. Overlooks the entrance road, with some vista points and quiet, tree-shaded sections.

Bath Path: 0.2 mile. 20-foot elevation change. Connects Spiritual Path to hot baths and sun deck area.

Village Path: 0.5 mile. 30-foot elevation change. Connects sun deck area to creekside camping and RV area.

Hot Baths, Swimming Pool and Sun Deck: After each hike, relax in multiple pools and on a large, partially shaded sun deck adjoining the lodge and dining room building.

Soak and Sleep

Hot mineral pools and all forms of overnight accommodations except RV hook-ups are available on the premises. If desired, your travel agent can secure motel accomodations in Middletown, which is five miles away.

▲ This tiled pool is the newest of the several pools in the garden complex adjoining the deck and swimming pool.

▲ A few yards from the warmest soaking pool, pipes from a cold water spring feed this invigorating plunge.

▲ Thanks to the clothing optional policy, this nursing mother can also soak and visit with friends at the same time.

▲ Accommodations on the premises
include rooms in the various buildings,
RV spaces with hookups and tent
◄ platforms in the camping area near the creek.

SUGARLOAF RIDGE STATE PARK

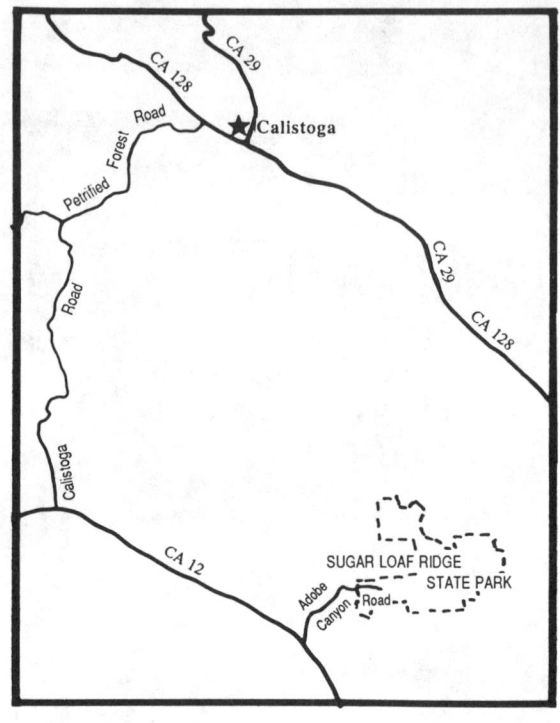

Location Overview

This day trip starts at Sugarloaf Ridge State Park, which covers 2,700 acres straddling the Mayacamas Mountains between the Sonoma and Napa Valleys. It ends 20 miles away in the northern end of the Napa Valley at the town of Calistoga, which is famous for its many mineral-water spas. The best weather at Sugarloaf is during spring and fall; the stream may slow to a trickle in the summer. Elevation: 600 to 2,700 feet.

The available activities are primarily hiking, stream play and meadow games at Sugarloaf, plus mineral-water soaking pools, mud baths, and other spa services at Calistoga.

Within Sugarloaf Ridge State Park there are 50 tree-shaded camp sites. Motels and RV parks are available within 15 miles. It is 15 miles to Santa Rosa Airport and 15 miles to Warrack Hospital, (707) 542-9030.

Tourist Attractions

Talk to your travel agent or contact the **Calistoga Chamber of Commerce, 1458 Lincoln Avenue, #4, Calistoga, CA 94515.**

▲ This entrance sign shows where park property includes the heavily wooded lower portion of Adobe Creek canyon.

▲ From this vista point on the Hillside Trail, miles of partially-wooded slopes invite further exploration.

▲ Lush meadows and miles of shade trees line both banks of Adobe Creek.

Trail Maps

This section identifies only a few of the available activities available at Sugarloaf and does not attempt to provide a detailed trail map. Therefore, you will need an official map of Sugarloaf Ridge State Park, and we recommend that you obtain it ahead of time by mail. Send your request with $1.00 to Sugarloaf Ridge State Park, 2605 Adobe Canyon Road, Kenwood, CA 95452, (707) 833-5712.

Topography and History

The ridge that identifies this park was named "Sugarloaf" before the turn of the century when sugar was sent to stores in loaves that looked like upside-down ice cream cones. Sonoma Creek begins in the park and runs for three miles through its southern portion. It is too shallow for swimming and often dries up by late summer, but it offers excellent safe stream play for families.

The park land includes three distinct ecological systems, chaparral-covered ridges, oak/fir forestland along the open meadows, and redwood forest in the canyon of Sonoma Creek. Summers at Sugarloaf Ridge are hot and dry. High temperatures are often in the 90s, but the evenings usually cool down into the 40s. Ocean fog sometimes penetrates this far inland. Most of the park's 40 inches of rain falls between November and April. Light snow occurs occasionally. Wintertime temperatures drop into the 30s at night, with daytime highs in the 50s and 60s. In the spring the park comes alive with wildflowers.

The Wappo Indian village of Wilikos was located here at the headwaters of Sonoma Creek before the first Spanish settlers came to California. The Wappo resisted Spanish intrusion more strongly than some other Indian groups. Their name is a corruption of the Spanish word guappo, which means "brave" or "daring." Even though the Indians were successful in resisting military takeover, their numbers were sharply reduced by the disastrous cholera epidemic of 1833 and the equally terrible smallpox epidemic of 1838. Most of those who survived were eventually relocated to the Mendocino Indian Reservation.

American settlers who came early to California were more interested in the fertile land of the valleys, but by the 1860s and '70s some of the later arrivals had settled in the hills near Sugarloaf Ridge where farming was limited and marginal. The State bought the property in 1920 in order to dam the creek and provide water for Sonoma State Hospital. In 1964 the land became part of the state park system.

▲ Well-marked trails allow individuals or small groups to hike with confidence.

▲ Native deer are protected from hunting, so they often approach within camera range, but are too shy to be touched.

▼ Bicycles are permitted on the paved perimeter road around the main meadow.

▲ All of the campsites are under the trees surrounding the vast main meadow.

Available Activities

This day-trip program is designed to include at least a soak in one of the Calistoga spa pools at the end of a day spent in Sugarloaf Ridge State Park. Your day-trip plans should be adjusted to fit current weather conditions and the physical abilities of the individuals in your group. Discuss your plans with a ranger when you arrive at the park in case one or more of the suggested activities should be changed for your comfort and convenience.

If you choose to reserve additional spa services in Calistoga, you will need to leave Sugarloaf in time to keep your Calistoga appointments. Make your choices accordingly.

Things to bring to Sugarloaf: sturdy walking shoes, layered clothing, swimsuit, sunscreen, insect repellant, first aid kit, towel, water, lunch, camera.

Trail surfaces are classified as follows:

Class 1: Generally smooth with no irregularities higher than a standard stair step (nine inches).

Class 2: Some irregularities higher than one stair step but none more than two stair steps (18 inches).

▲ After carrying rushing runoff from winter storms, spring-fed Adobe Creek gradually slows to a trickle by August.

57 SUGARLOAF RIDGE STATE PARK

▲ Families like these creekside picnic areas because parents can easily watch children playing in the nearby water.

▶ The Hillside Trail has this vista point but the longer trails to the higher mountains have even grander vistas.

▼ Wading barefoot through a sandy-bottom pool of fresh water has a special magic value for children who live in the city.

Creekside Nature Trail Loop: 1.1 miles. Minor elevation change. Class 1 surface. The numbered posts along the trail correspond to numbered paragraphs of descriptive information in the official park map.

Hillside Trail/Meadow Trail Loop: 2.6 miles. 400-foot elevation change. Class 1 surface except for a few Class 2 spots. Some steep sections at the start, leading to a vista point and then an easy return through a meadow.

Pony Gate / Canyon Trail Loop: 4.0 miles. 400-foot elevation change. Class 1 surface except for some Class 2 spots in the canyon. Several steep sections and many trees.

▼ Steam from the source spring can be seen spouting into the air at the end of this huge Indian Springs swimming pool.

▲ This mineral water pool area at Calistoga Spa Hot Springs offers a variety of depths and temperatures, including a large covered pool.

Day-Use Hot Pools (Calistoga): On busy weekends these spas may close their pools to use by non-registered guests, so phone first: Calistoga Spa, (707) 942-6269; Dr. Wilkinson's, (707) 942-4702; Le Spa Francais, (707) 942-4636; Nance's, (707) 942-6211.

Day-Use Swimming Pool (Calistoga): Indian Springs Pool, (707) 942-4913. 1712 Lincoln Avenue. Olympic-size swimming pool with natural mineral water maintained at 85 to 95 degrees. Ideal for kids.

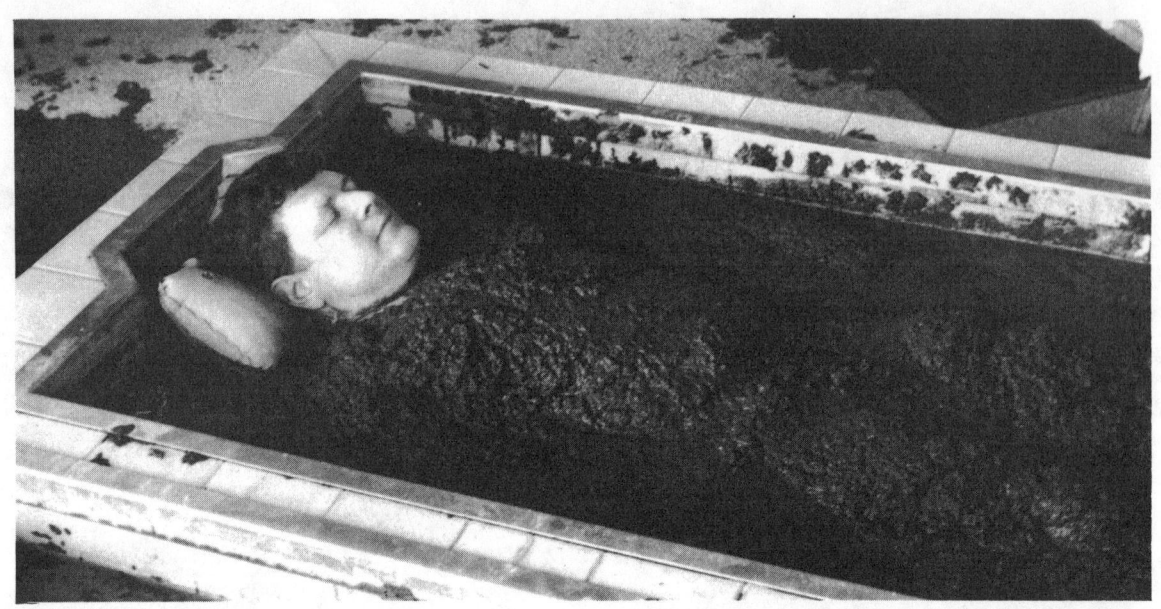

▼ Individual hydrojet tubs are part of the specialized fitness equipment in the men's bathhouse at Calistoga Spa.

▲ This mud is not just ordinary dirt. Each bathhouse claims to have the best combination of mudbath ingredients.

Spa services (mud bath, massage, etc.) in separate men's and women's bathhouses (Calistoga): Phone any of the above-listed locations for appointments.

Spa services for couples (Calistoga): Enzyme soak, mud bath, massage, etc. Phone International Spa for appointment, (707) 942-6122.

▲ Spa service for couples is a recent innovation, rapidly becoming popular.

▼ Campers are able to have safe outdoor fires in these large metal firepits.

MUD BATHS FOR COUPLES

ENZYME BATHS FROM JAPAN

EUROPEAN HERBAL BATH TREATMENTS

HERBAL FACIALS

HERBAL BLANKET WRAPS

ACUPRESSURE MASSAGE

FOOT REFLEXOLOGY

Soak and Sleep

Sugarloaf Ridge State Park has 50 tree-shaded sites surrounding a very large meadow. Reservations are recommended except in winter. Contact MISTIX, (800) 444-7275 from within California; (619) 452-1950 from outside California.

Spa Hotels in Calistoga: All of the spas listed above under <u>Day-Use Hot Pools</u> offer rooms. Phone for information on rates and reservations.

BIG BEND HOT SPRINGS

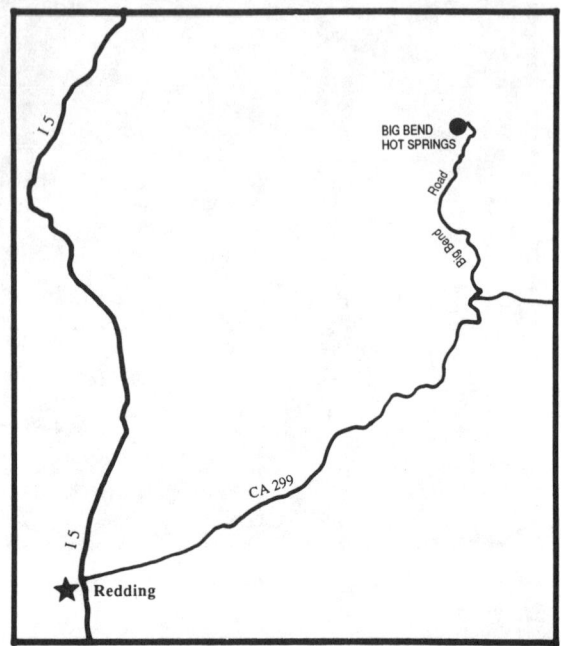

Location Overview

This peaceful 100-acre, private, rustic retreat is located on the Pit River, has three hot springs, and is surrounded by Shasta National Forest. Open all year. Elevation 1,700 feet.

Available activities include hiking, river floating, hot-pool digging and hot pool soaking.

Overnight camping sites and cabins are available on the premises. The location also includes a variety of primitive and improved soaking pools. It is 35 miles to a motel, 60 miles to Redding Municipal Airport, and 60 miles to Redding Medical Center, (619) 244-5400.

● ● ● ● ● ● ● ● ● ● ● ● ● ● ● ● ● ● ● ●

Tourist Attractions

Talk to your travel agent or contact the Redding Visitors Bureau, 77 Auditorium Drive, Redding, CA 96002, (916) 225-4100.

● ● ● ● ● ● ● ● ● ● ● ● ● ● ● ● ● ● ● ●

▲ The water temperature in this cliffside soaking pool can be controlled by adding cold water whenever desired.

▲ Many centuries ago spring floods carved this valley, but the construction of power dams has now tamed the Pit River.

◀ This warm soaking pool at the edge of the river is supplied by one of the three hot springs at this location.

Trail Maps

A trail map is not needed for this location. However, we suggest that you obtain information about the organization that owns and operates the site. Send your request to Big Bend Hot Springs, 196 Hot Springs Row, Big Bend, CA 96011, (916) 337-6680.

▲ More than 50 gallons per minute of 180-degree water flows out of the river bank just above the riverbed rocks.

Topography and History

Massive geologic forces have been working on this area for millions of years. Sedimentary layers have been uplifted by granite intrusions, volcanic lava flows have covered thousands of square miles, and ice age glaciers have gouged out hundreds of valleys. Before the Pit River was tamed by a series of power company dams, it carved deeply and carried massive erosion debris as it drained the great lava plain. During recent millenia, streams have collected decomposed rock and organic fragments to form meadows and rolling hills which are now covered with conifer forests and mantles of manzanita.

During the periods of major geologic activity in the area, extremes of heat and pressure concentrated and refined many mineral deposits. A ten-year boom was set off by the discovery of gold in 1848, followed by the establishment of silver and iron mines. A copper boom started around the turn of the century, and timber harvesting became a growing industry during the same period. The collapse of copper prices in 1920 caused a local depression, which lasted until the construction of Shasta Dam (1938-1945), and the filling of Shasta Lake. Tourist recreation has now become a major part of the local economy.

Before the arrival of white explorers and settlers, the large and peaceful Wintu Indian tribe enjoyed unlimited access to the forests, rivers, fish, game, fowls, roots and grass. Their tepees of grass and brush were usually built facing nearby Mt. Shasta where the Great Spirit dwelt in his stone house. Game was trapped in pits dug in the earth some feet deep and several feet across. Narrowing at the top and covered with light brush, grass and leaves, these pits were the source of the name for the Pit River.

The intrusion of prospectors and settlers into the area brought on escalating cycles of friendship, betrayal, fear and hostility, all too familiar in other states. Assassinations, lynchings, ranch burnings, militia raids, tribal war parties, etc., punctuated the seizure of Indian hunting grounds by saoldiers and settlers. After the Indians were decimated by disease and their warriors outgunned, they were herded eventually into the present pattern of reservations.

The wet and dry seasons are strongly delineated in Shasta County. Rains begin around October and continue somewhat erratically through May and June. June and July are the dry months of higher temperatures, though it is not unusual to have rain in either of these months. Spring and fall are the delightful seasons. The fall is called "California's second spring." Snow falls during the winter months on the mountains and insures plenty of water in the creeks for summer use. Snow sometimes visits the valley and nearby foothills in limited depths that soon melt.

▲ Ice age glaciers scraped through valleys in this area and left scattered piles of debris as they gradually melted away.

▲ Stopping to pick wild berries in season is easy when you dawdle and meander along Old Fisherman's Trail.

Available Activities

Your day-trip plans should be adjusted to fit current weather conditions and the physical abilities of the individuals in your group. Discuss them at the office when you arrive in case one or more of the suggested activities should be changed for your comfort and convenience.

Things to bring: layered clothing, sturdy walking shoes, sunscreen, insect repellant, first aid kit, towel, water, lunch, camera, small inflatable raft.

The one available trail has a Class 1 surface, which means there are no irregularities higher than a standard stair step (nine inches). The following suggested day trip program will provide a variety of environments:

Old Fisherman's Trail: Suggested maximum, 5 miles round trip. Minor elevation change. This old PG&E service road through the trees along the river bank gradually narrows to an overgrown path. Seldom used, quiet and peaceful.

River Floating: 0.25 mile from campground. 40 foot elevation change. River flow is usually deep enough to float a small raft, but not too deep to get out and walk. Excellent when alternated with soaks in the nearby hot pools.

The flow rate of the Pit River is controlled by a series of upriver PG&E power dams so there isn't enough water for spectacular white water rafting.

▲ Instead of bracing for exciting plunges through turbulent rapids, these rafters can relax and drift with the current.

▼ Whenever the passengers have seen enough scenery they can paddle to shore and carry the raft back for another trip.

67 BIG BEND HOT SPRINGS

▲ Volunteers are continually rearranging the rocks to create more, larger, deeper, and better soaking pools. Their creativity is unlimited because the size and supply of rocks is unlimited.

River Bank Hot Pools: 0.25 mile from campground. 40 foot elevation change. Scalding (180-degree) spring water flows from a spring through acres of uneven flood plain and rocks toward the stream, cooling as it goes. Volunteers have built, and are welcome to improve, a series of primitive soaking pools that have different temperatures.

▲ Scalding water from the river bank spring gradually cools as it flows through the rocks toward the river. Volunteers have excavated soaking pools at various places along that path, trying for just the right temperature.

▲ This is one of the rock and cement temperature-controllable soaking pools which has a fine view of the river.

Soak and Sleep

Ten camping sites and three cabins are available on the premises. Natural mineral water is piped to three indoor, individual soaking tubs and four outdoor, rock-and-cement soaking pools overlooking the river. Cold spring water is piped to each of the outdoor pools so that pool temperatures may be controlled.

Charm Motel: (916) 335-2254.
P.O. Box 266, Burney, CA 96013. Offering 30 units on tree-shaded grounds.

Best Western Hilltop Inn: (916) 221-6100.
2300 Hilltop Drive, Redding, CA 96002. Offering 113 rooms, restaurant, swimming pool and hydropool.

COTTONWOOD CAMPGROUND

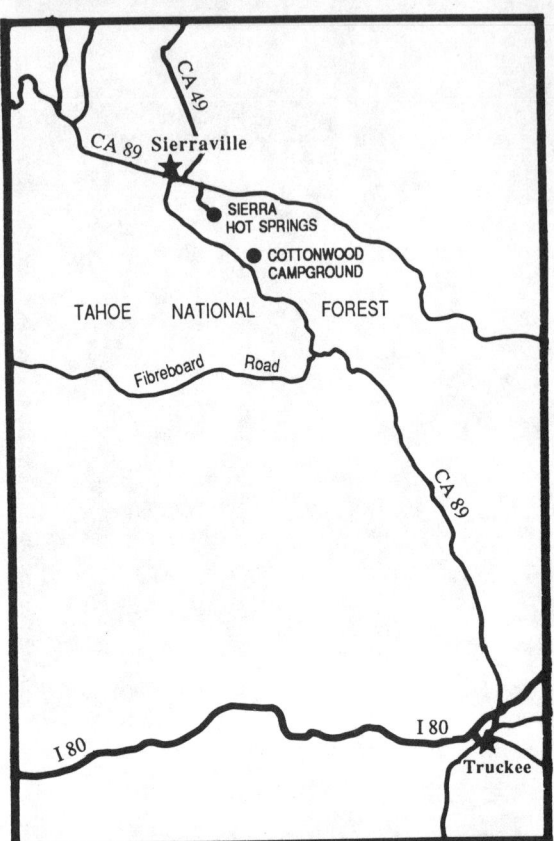

Location Overview

This family campground is one of dozens in the 800,000-acre Tahoe National Forest. It has a creek and several nature trails and is less than ten miles from Sierra Hot Springs. It is usable year-round except during rain or winter snow season. Elevation: 5,000 feet.

The available activities are primarily hiking and fishing. There is an excellent self-guided botanical trail but no visitor center. No bicycles are permitted on trails. Horses are permitted on nearby Mt. Lola trail only.

Campsites at this campground may be reserved through MISTIX. It is five miles to a hotel or motel and seven miles to hot spring soaking pools. It is 45 miles to Reno Airport and 18 miles to Sierra Valley District Hospital, (916) 993-1225.

Tourist Attractions

Talk to your travel agent or contact the Sierra County Chamber of Commerce, P.O. Box 222, Downieville, CA 95936. (916) 289-3122.

▲ At Sierra Hot Springs, natural mineral water can be enjoyed in this very civilized redwood tub and deck.

▲ Along the Botanical Nature Trail, shady spots in the meadow invite all passersby to recline and relax for a while.

Trail Maps

This section identifies only a few of the activities available and does not attempt to provide a detailed trail map. Therefore, you will need an official recreation map of the Tahoe National Forest, and we suggest that you obtain it ahead of time by mail. Send your request with $2.00 to Sierraville Ranger District, P.O. Box 95, Sierraville, CA 96126, (916) 994-3401. Be sure to mention Cottonwood Campground and ask for supplementary information about your areas of special interest, such as campgrounds, trails, fishing, equestrian facilities, bicycle routes, etc.

▲ Along the rugged Mt. Lola Trail mighty stumps inspire at least a mighty yell.

▲ Lush alpine-stream undergrowth surrounds this bridge on the Fisherman's Trail.

Topography and History

Thousands of years ago glaciers scoured alpine valleys into a vast range of granite mountains, now called the Sierra Nevada. Centuries of winter snow and spring runoff have carved deep canyons, created dozens of lakes, and deposited top soil in the alpine valleys. As the climate warmed, vegetation thrived, including mountain chaparral, mixed conifers, alpine plants, lodgepole pine, pinyon-juniper and sage bitterbrush. Eventually, forested areas grew to include ponderosa pine, sugar pine, Jeffrey pine, Douglas fir, white fir, red fir and incense cedar.

The name "Tahoe" is derived from a Washoe Indian word meaning "Big Water," a fitting name for famous Lake Tahoe, which straddles the California-Nevada Border and is the name source for the Tahoe National Forest. During the 1800s the seemingly endless resources of the region were exploited without regard for ecological consequences. The western slopes still bear scars from the frenzy of gold rush days, when large-scale hydraulic and hard-rock mining was added to the early practice of placer mining with pan and sluice box. The introduction of sheep and cattle led to uncontrolled overgrazing, and the growth of cities stimulated uncontrolled timber-cutting. By the turn of the century, this destructive depletion of public land and resources led to the creation of the National Forest system and a more balanced management of the "land of many uses."

During the gold rush days, some of California's new residents arrived via clipper ship around Cape Horn, but most had to find a way over the Sierra Nevada range when there were no interstate highways. The history of the mountain passes traversed by these newcomers is full of heroic tales, awesome difficulties and some terrible tragedies. On Hwy 89 three miles north of Truckee there is a short self-guided path through the campsite of the ill-fated Donner party.

During the 1900s the snow-catching potential of the Sierra Nevada mountains has become the all-important water source for millions of acres of Central Valley cropland and for millions of residents in the western California counties and the Nevada cities to the east. As a result, the task of the National Forest Service has been expanded to include watershed protection and management of recreation areas around the reservoirs created by Reclamation Bureau dams.

Available Activities

Your day-trip plans should be adjusted to fit current weather conditions and the physical abilities of the individuals in your group. Discuss your plans with a ranger when you arrive in case one or more of the suggested activities should be changed for your comfort and convenience.

Things to bring: sturdy walking shoes, layered clothing, swimsuit, sunscreen, insect repellant, first aid kit, towel, water, lunch, camera.

Trail surfaces are classified as follows:
Class 1: Generally smooth with no irregularities higher than a standard stair step (nine inches).
Class 2. Some irregularities higher than a standard stair step, but none higher than two stair steps (18 inches).
Class 3: Some irregularities higher than 18 inches.

The trails around Cottonwood Campground can be easily explored in one day and are described below as a suggested day-trip program. For the more ambitious hiker, a longer nearby trail is described as an alternate program:

 In contrast, pine trees and bare rocks dominate the landscape along the Mt. Lola Trail, far above running streams.

Cottonwood Nature Trail/Fisherman Trail: 0.5-mile loop. 15 foot elevation change. Class 1 surface. Smooth and easy self-guided botanical trail that winds through pine and aspen trees and along the bank of Cottonwood Creek.

Overlook Trail: 2 miles round trip. 500-foot elevation change. Class 1 surface. Well-marked trail through brush and forests, with some switchbacks, to a panoramic view at the top. Take plenty of water and plan to rest often at this altitude.

▲
▼ Starting from the campground, the easy self-guided Botanical Trail dawdles and meanders through forests and meadows.

▲ Educational information on a printed flyer corresponds to the numbered posts set out along the Botanical Trail.

The Overlook Trail also starts from the campground, but climbs rapidly toward a rocky peak with a panoramic view.

Thoughtful woodcutters have left tree sections to serve as handy seats for winded visitors on the Overlook Trail.

The upper reaches of the Mt. Lola Trail are rocky, dry and hot in the summer, ideal for tough hikers and equestrians.

Alternate day trip program:

Mt. Lola Trail: 12 miles roundtrip. 2,500 foot elevation change. Class 1 and 2 surface. The lower portion of this trail follows a creek through thick forests and open meadows, but it is definitely uphill, and loose gravel on some of the steep sections provides uncertain footing. Take plenty of water, rest often, and be prepared to start back down whenever the trip becomes more work than fun.

Directions (from Cottonwood Campground): Drive four miles south on Hwy 89; turn right (west) on Forest Service Road #07 for 1.3 miles. Turn left (south) on Independence Lake Road for 0.25 mile to junction with Sierra County Road #S301. Turn right (west) for 3 miles to the unmarked trailhead.

The lower reaches of the Mt. Lola Trail run through cooler and more enjoyable forests, meadows, and a creek.

▲
▼ At Sierra Hot Springs there is a variety of soaking pools, including an urban-type redwood pool with deck and a ranch-type cattle-watering trough.

▲ Continuous flow-through maintains different temperatures in each of the three sections of this cement pool.

Soak and Sleep

Cottonwood Campground has 49 reservable sites; phone MISTIX (800) 444-PARK, from within California; (619) 452-1950 from outside California.

Canyon Ranch Resort: (916) 994-3340
P.O. Box 6, Sierraville, CA 96126. Offering eight completely- furnished cabins. Pool and spa available during summer months.

Sierra Hot Springs: (916) 994-3773.
P.O. Box 366, Sierraville, CA 96126. Several different outdoor soaking pools with various temperatures are available in 1991 to the public, at or near the spring outlets. Starting in 1992, several indoor soaking pools and an outdoor swimming pool will be available. Also in 1992, rooms will be available in the lodge on the spring property, and in a hotel two miles away in Sierraville. Telephone for rates, reservations, directions, and the current status of planned additional construction.

GROVER HOT SPRINGS STATE PARK

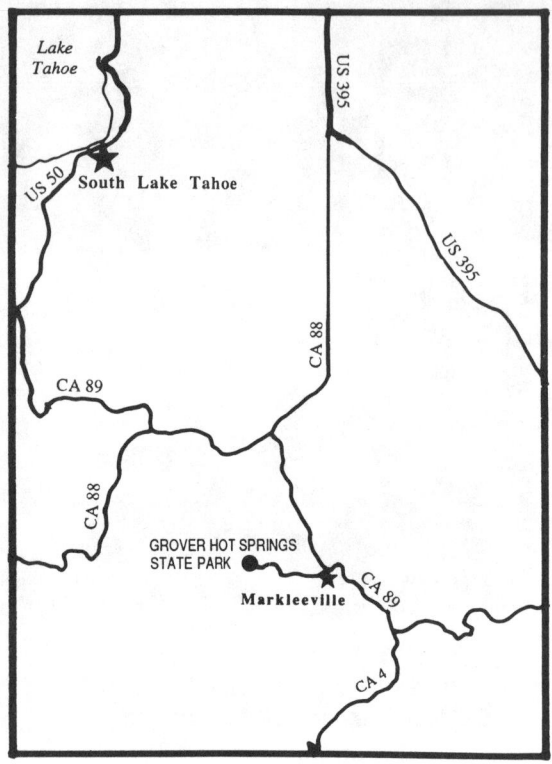

Location Overview

Tourist Attractions

Talk to your travel agent or contact the Alpine County Chamber of Commerce, P.O. Box 265, Department G, Markleeville, CA 96120, (916) 694-2475.

This 500-acre park includes a classic alpine meadow surrounded by forests and high mountain peaks. The hot pools, which are open all year, attract Nordic skiers in the winter. Elevation: 6,000 feet.

The summer activities are primarily hiking and fishing. There is an excellent self-guided nature trail through the meadow, but no visitor center.

The campsites within the park are closed from October to May, but winter camping is permitted in the adjoining picnic area. It is 4 miles to food and lodging in Markleeville. It is 85 miles to Reno Airport and 40 miles to Barton Memorial Hospital, (916) 541-3420.

▲ The Grover Hot Springs pools are on the south edge of a huge alpine meadow surrounded by delightful pine forests.

◄ The Burnside Lake Trail rises out of the meadow into massive rock formations.

Trail Maps

This section does not attempt to provide a detailed trail map. Therefore, you will need an official map of Grover Hot Springs State Park, and we recommend that you obtain it ahead of time by mail. Send your request with 25 cents to Grover Hot Springs State Park, P.O. Box 188, Markleeville, CA 96120, (916) 694-2248.

▲ A few hardy trees have managed to find footing and nourishment among the rocks.

Topography and History

The 519-acre park lies in Hot Springs Valley at an elevation of 6,000 feet, with mountains rising abruptly on three sides. Hawkins Peak, at 10,023 feet, is three miles northwest of the valley; Markleeville Peak, at 9,417 feet, lies four miles to the southwest.

Ever since the mid 1850s, when journalists began putting into words their impressions of Grover Hot springs, the descriptions have been generous. The area is one of alpine beauty with a large variety of plant and animal life.

The park's hot springs are a phenomenon associated with the faulting that developed when the Sierra Nevada began to rise millions of years ago. Surface water that courses its way through the cracks in the earth's crust reaches hot rock thousands of feet below and then then bubbles to the surface, dissolving minerals along the way. For many years before the advent of modern medicine, people sought the curative powers they believed existed in the waters of Grover Hot Springs. The springs, they said, cured a long list of chronic illnesses.

One of the park's two concrete pools is fed by runoff from six mineral springs. Although the water leaves the ground at 148 degrees, the pools inflow is regulated so the temperature remains between 102 and 104 degrees in the hot pool. Excess water and overflow from the pools are diverted into nearby Hot Springs Creek, a year-round stream that flows through the middle of the park's large meadow. Pool hours depend on the season; call the park for them when you plan to visit.

During the summer months, the nighttime temperature at the park drops to around 50 degrees, and the daytime reading reaches around 80. Frost is not uncommon in early June and may come again in late August or early September, when the colder weather brings a rich display of orange and gold in stands of quaking aspen.

Visitors can fish the creek during the summer months. Catchable-size trout are planted periodically as long as the creek maintains an adequate waterflow. Four miles east of the park is the Carson River, and farther upstream is Silver Creek, both noted for their excellent trout fishing.

▲▼ These visitors are enjoying an alpine meadow and a pine forest without first back packing uphill for two days.

Available Activities

Your day-trip plans should be adjusted to fit current weather conditions and the physical abilities of the individuals in your group. Discuss your plans with a ranger when you arrive in case one or more of the suggested activities should be changed for your comfort and convenience.

Things to bring: sturdy walking shoes, layered clothing, swimsuit, sunscreen, insect repellant, first aid kit, towel, water, lunch, camera.

Trail surfaces are classified as follows:

Class 1: Generally smooth with no irregularities higher than a standard stair step (nine inches).

Class 2: Some irregularities higher than one stair step, but none higher than two stair steps (18 inches).

3. Some irregularities higher than 18 inches.

The following suggested day-trip program will provide examples of several different environments:

"Transition Walk" Nature Trail Loop: (Printed pamphlets describing the area's natural history are available at the park office.) 1.025 miles. 20 foot elevation change. Class 1 surface. This is a smooth path along the stream and around the north half of the meadow.

Hot Springs Trail: 0.6 miles. 20 foot elevation change. Class 1 surface. A smooth path through the south half of the meadow, connecting the hot pools and the campground area.

During the summer there are guided walks, printed pamphlets are available for the self-guided nature trail, and everyone is free to dawdle and meander.

▲ The waterfall trail delivers the wide open spaces, including smogless air, blue sky, pine trees and big rocks.

Burnside Lake Trail to Waterfall: 3.5 miles round trip. 200 foot elevation change. Class 1 surface while going through the pine trees, with some Class 2 sections in the rock outcroppings near the waterfall.

▲ High altitude hiking can be breathtaking. Plan to sit and rest often.

◄ Don't forget your camera. This delicate waterfall tumbing over a giant rock invites inspection and recording.

83 GROVER HOT SPRINGS

▲
▼ The Hot Springs Creek water in the pool (above) flows through a gap in the rocks and comes out (below) as a waterfall.

▲ Some visitors claim that these rocks are a free-form jungle gym, 20 miles long.

Soak and Sleep

A fee is charged for entry into the pools. Phone (916) 694-2248 for current fee schedule. For safety reasons, the number of people in the hot pools at any one time is limited by the lifeguard in attendance. You may have to stand in a waiting line if you arrive between mid-morning and late afternoon. Therefore, it is advisable to go for an early morning soak, hike the suggested trails until late afternoon, and then return to the hot pools for a day-ending soak.

Each of the 76 campsites is equipped with stoves, cupboards and tables, and is close to piped water and restrooms with showers. Reservations are required. Call MISTIX, (800) 446-7275 from within California; (619) 452-1950 from outside California. The campground area is closed from early October to May, but winter camping is permitted in the picnic area adjacent to the park entrance.

Alpine Hotel & Cutthroat Saloon: (916) 694-2150. P.O. Box 261, Markleeville, CA 96120. Five miles from the park. Offering ten rooms, bar and restaurant.

Woodfords Inn: (916) 694-2150. P.O. Box 426, Markleeville, CA 96120. Twelve miles from the park, at the junction of Hwys 88 and 89. Offering 20 rooms and a hydropool.

Sorenson's Resort: (916) 694-2203. 14255 Hwy 88, Hope Valley, CA 96120. Fifteen miles from the park. Offering 23 rustic cabins, restaurant, sauna.

▲ The lifeguard's office is between the warm pool in the foreground and the cooler swimming pool in the background.

▲ The people on the hill are looking at the source spring which supplies hot mineral water to the soaking pool below.

BUCKEYE HOT SPRINGS

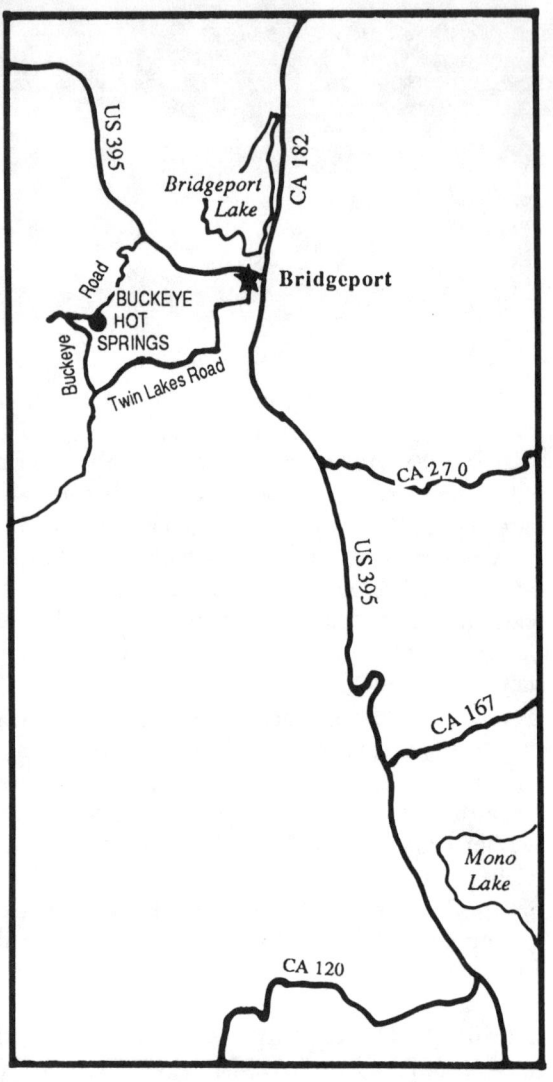

Location Overview

These Toiyabe National Forest hot springs flow into Buckeye Creek on the eastern slopes of the Sierra Nevada, ten miles west of Bridgeport. The suggested day-trip program includes hiking on the Buckeye Creek Trail and visiting Travertine Hot Springs south of Bridgeport. the Buckeye Hot Springs area is not accessible by road during winter snow season. Elevation: 6,800 feet.

Available activities include hiking, fishing, and hot pool soaking. Mountain bikes and saddle horses are permitted on some trails.

There is a creekside National Forest campground one mile from the hot springs. Motels and RV parks are available ten miles away in Bridgeport. It is 100 miles to Cannon International (Reno) Airport and 13 miles to Mono Emergency Room, (702) 932-7011.

Tourist Attractions

Talk to your travel agent or contact the Bridgeport Chamber of Commerce, P.O. Box 541, Bridgeport, CA 93417, (619) 932-7033.

Trail Maps

This section identifies only a few of the available activities in this region and does not attempt to provide a detailed trail map. Therefore, you will need an official map of Toiyabe National Forest, and we recommend that you obtain it ahead of time by mail. Send your request for the Bridgeport Ranger District map with $3.12 to Bridgeport Ranger District, P.O. Box 595, Bridgeport, CA 93517, (619) 932-7070.

 Melted snow in Buckeye Creek flows through this beautiful canyon. The soaking pools are in the foreground.

▲ Buckeye Creek Trail is designated for use by equestrians as well as by hikers.

Topography and History

The eastern front of the Sierra Nevada range in the vicinity of Mt. Whitney rises higher above its immediate surroundings than any other mountain front in the United States. This front is slightly less impressive in the Toiyabe National Forest but is, nevertheless, a massive wall of mountains.

This abrupt rise in elevation resulted from millions of years of geologic sculpturing of the earth's surface. Volcanic flows combined with the uplifting, folding and faulting of the earth's crust form the mold of the Sierra Nevada. It was then left to the glaciers of the Ice Age to add the finishing touch. The glacial moraines and lake-filled basins in the Bridgeport District are classic examples.

The volcanoes that helped build this area no longer spout lava, but the presence of molten rock close to the earth's surface is indicated by the dozens of fumeroles and hot springs scattered along a major fault at the base of the mountains. Small earthquakes accompanying subterranean earth movement are almost continuous. When underground channels carrying geothermal water are changed by this movement, some hot springs may cease to flow, and new springs may begin to flow nearby.

The Sierra Nevada range was first crossed by Jedediah Smith in 1827. John Fremont crossed the Sierra in 1843-44 and kept an accurate record of his journey. Fremont succeeded in crossing the main summit of the Sierra via Carson Pass in 1844.

The Indians Fremont encountered were members of the Paiute and Washoe tribes. The Washoe Indians roamed the eastern Sierra Nevada as far south as the Sonora Pass. The Paiute Indians lived farther south on the eastern slopes of the Sierra and in the western valleys of the Great Basin. The name "Toiyabe" is of Indian origin, a Shoshone word for "black mountains."

▲ Centuries of mineral water flow and evaporation have built the large tufa formation which hangs over the creek.

The first substantial gold rush on the eastern slope of the Sierra Nevada was at Dogtown and Monoville in 1859. This eventually led to mining on a grand scale in such booming centers as Aurora, Bodie, Lundy and Masonic. Many fortunes were made and lost in these early stampedes to the silver and gold camps. Bodie, now a ghost town popular with tourists, was one of the wildest of the western mining camps.

Snow begins to accumulate at the higher elevations in October and closes unplowed roads at 7,000 feet for the winter months, sometimes lasting through late spring. Daytimes are cool, even during summer months, and nighttime temperatures may drop into the 40s. During the summer, afternoon thunderstorms may deliver torrential rains on short notice. Inquire at the Bridgeport Ranger Station for current weather conditions.

▲ Part of the Buckeye Creek Trail runs through large groves of green trees.

▲ What you see is what you get. Buckeye Creek is an authentic mountain stream offering both beauty and good fishing.

▲ Along the Buckeye Creek Trail there are plenty of boulders suitable for sitting and watching the clouds drift by.

Available Activities

Your day-trip plans should be adjusted to fi current weather conditions and the physical abilitie of the individuals in your group.

Discuss them with rangers at the Bridgeport Range Station when you arrive, in case one or more of the suggested activities should be changed for you comfort and convenience.

Things to bring: layered clothing, including rai gear, sturdy walking shoes, sunscreen, insec repellant, first aid kit, water, lunch, towel, camera.

The surfaces of all suggested trails are Class I which means there are no irregularities higher tha a standard stair step (nine inches).

Toiyabe National Forest offers far more hikin trails than can be explored in one day. Th following suggested day trip program provide activities in the immediate vicinity of Buckeye H Springs:

Buckeye Creek Trail to Big Meadow: 7. miles round trip. 400 foot elevation change. Eas gradual uphill walk on road-width trail through pir trees and chaparral to large alpine meadov Mountain bikes and saddle horses are permitted. B sure to close the private property gate after yc have opened it to go through.

▲
▶ Portions of the Buckeye Creek Trail run through sunny open spaces away from the thick underbrush on the creek banks.

▲ The trail rejoins the creek when it reaches the big meadow, just in time to provide welcome relief for tired feet.

91 BUCKEYE HOT SPRINGS

Travertine Hot Springs: Ten miles by vehicle from Buckeye Hot Springs. A picturesque cluster of sporadic hot springs with volunteer-built soaking pools offer a choice of temperatures and views. Directions: From Bridgeport, drive 0.6 mile south on US 395 and turn east on paved Jack Sawyer Road. Within the next 0.3 mile there are three unmarked forks. At the first fork (on the left), keep going straight. At the second fork, where the paved road goes off to the right, keep going straight on the dirt road. At the third fork (on the left), bear right on the road that winds up into the hills. Drive 0.4 mile to the fourth fork (on the left, signed *Bridgeport Borrow Pit*). Continue straight ahead for 0.7 mile to a parking area near the large soaking pool. To reach the series of volunteer-built pools, walk downhill 100 yards southwest.

▲ ▼ The white formation near this Travertine Hot Springs soaking pool is a geothermal tufa mound, built by centuries of mineral water outflow and evaporation.

▲ Volunteers have built this creek-edge pool to efficiently mix 135-degree mineral water with freezing creek water.

◄ In addition to the creekside pool, there is this small two-person pool which overlooks the creek and the valley.

Buckeye Hot Springs: One mile downstream from Buckeye Campground and 100 yards downstream from the bridge over Buckeye Creek. Two primitive volunteer-built soaking pools, with a tradition of clothing optional, offer a unique opportunity to interact with nature.

Soak and Sleep

Buckeye Campground, one mile upstream from the hot springs, is open May to October on a first-come/first-served basis. There is also a large level space near the Buckeye Creek bridge where overnight parking is not prohibited.

Bridgeport Inn: (619) 932-7380.
Main Street, Bridgeport, CA 93417. Offering 35 motel units, plus bar and restaurant.

MAMMOTH MOUNTAIN BIKE PARK

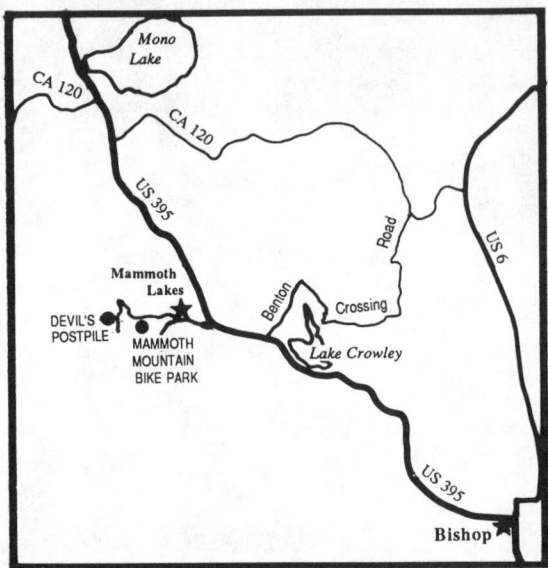

Location Overview

This famous ski mountain is located on the east slope of the Sierra, just off US 395, 100 miles south of Lake Tahoe. During the summer it is converted into a versatile mountain-bike complex with 75 miles of roads and trails uncluttered by hikers, horses or vehicles. A ski-lift gondola is available to take you and your bike to the top, with unlimited repeat trips. Elevation: 9,000 to 11,000 feet.

Bike riding is the basic activity, but the variety of routes and surroundings, including a lovely lake, permits individual enjoyment of spectacular views, downhill speed runs, and forest dawdling.

Rooms are available at Mammoth Mountain Inn, across the street from the ski lifts. A National Forest campground, a commercial RV park and hydropool-equipped condominiums are available four miles away in the town of Mammoth Lakes. It is 15 miles to Mammoth-June airport and four miles to Centinela-Mammoth Hospital (619) 934-3311.

Coasting downhill through a forest with no vehicles, equestrians or hikers is what this specialized park is all about.

Tourist Attractions

Talk to your travel agent or contact the Mammoth Lakes Visitor Bureau, P.O. Box 48, Mammoth Lakes, CA 93546, (619) 934-2712.

▲ During the summer, ski lift gondolas give mountain bike riders an effortles lift to the top of the mountain.

Trail Maps

This section identifies only a few of the bike trails available and does not attempt to provide a detailed trail map. Therefore, you will need an official photo-map of Mammoth Mountain Bike Park, and we suggest that you obtain it ahead of time by mail. To request a free map, phone or write to Mammoth Adventure Connection, P.O. Box 353, Mammoth Lakes, CA 93546, (619) 934-0606. Be sure to ask for supplementary information about your areas of special interest, such as bike/lodging packages, guided orientation rides, bike rentals, racing and obstacle courses, van pick-up service, etc.

▲ Direction signs for bike trails get the same careful attention as do ski trails.

▲ During the last half of the two-stage hoist up the mountain, gondola riders get a dramatic view of the High Sierra.

▲ In the summit building, attendants detach the bikes from the gondolas and guide the riders to this exit door.

Topography and History

US 395 is the paved ribbon that runs through all of the valleys along "the back side of the Sierra," which catches the first rays of sunrise and the first shadows of afternoon. About 100 miles south of Lake Tahoe and 300 miles north of Los Angeles is the exit to the town of Mammoth Lakes and nearby Mammoth Mountain, a world-class ski resort.

During winter months in the high Sierra, the huge white dome of 11,000 foot Mammoth Mountain looks like the back of a mammoth white elephant among saber-toothed peaks. It is the blown-out side of an old volcano crater, which accounts for its unique appearance. It is also in just the right location to extract some extra snow out of every winter storm.

Until the middle of this century, Mammoth Mountain was just one of many ski-worthy slopes in the Inyo National Forest. Dave McCoy, a local ski instructor and portable rope-tow operator, was the first to recognize its superior potential. After the war, he installed the first permanent rope-tow and attracted an annually increasing number of skiers. In 1953 the Forest Service put the Mammoth Mountain ski resort permit out for bid and McCoy got it by default when there were no other applicants. McCoy's ability as a ski coach helped promote the reputation of Mammoth Mountain. Parents sent their children to be coached by Dave, and 19 of the racers he trained represented the United States on Olympic teams.

The first chairlift was built in 1955. McCoy's enterprise has now expanded to include 30 lifts, three large day lodges, a hotel property, two restaurants, a large maintenance facility and much more. During the summer of 1991, miles of pipes were installed to give Mammoth the ability to generate its own snow on some of the north slopes in the early fall and late spring, thereby extending the ski season.

Starting in 1990, Mammoth Mountain also began to offer a summer mountain bike season. Seventy five miles of roads and trails (most with less than six percent grade) have been constructed on the open upper slopes and through the trees of the lower slopes. Ski-lift gondolas have been fitted with racks so that bikes and riders may be effortlessly deposited on the top of the mountain, ready for a leisurely downhill coast.

During the summer of 1991, Mammoth Mountain Bike Park also constructed obstacle courses and other special facilities that were used during mountain bike World Cup competition. The fastest racer whizzed down the 3 1/2- mile Kamikaze Trail in just over five minutes, averaging more than 40 miles per hour.

The Bike Park staff has a policy of supporting and encouraging bike riders at all skill levels. In addition to renting bikes and selling lift tickets, they can provide daily orientations, advice on trail selection, instruction classes and guides for individuals or groups. They even provide van pick-up service along designated bike routes that extend more than a dozen miles beyond the boundaries of the Bike Park.

Available Activities

The suggested day-trip program for this location starts at the Mammoth Mountain Inn (across from the Bike Park office) and ends up at Hot Creek, 15 miles away. You can drive your car to Hot Creek, or you can ride your mountain bike (mostly downhill) to Hot Creek and then be picked up and returned to the Inn by a Bike Park van.

You day-trip plans should be chosen to fit current weather conditions and the physical abilities of the individuals in your group. Discuss your plans with Bike Park staff when you arrive in case one or more of the suggested activities should be changed for your comfort and convenience.

Things to bring: mountain bike and equipment (may also be rented), layered clothing, sunscreen, camera. Additional items for Hot Creek: towel, swimsuit, first aid kit.

All trails may be safely used if you control your speed. Designated Bike Park trails come in two widths, single-track and road. Passing is easier on road-width trails, but most of the wooded-area trails are single-track. This location is too large to be fully explored in one day. The following suggested day trip program will provide examples of several different environments:

▲ These riders are braking into the first big curve on the Kamikaze Trail after leaving the summit building (top left).

▼ The lodge and ski lift buildings are visible 2,000 feet below these riders who are on their third Kamikaze run.

From Mid-Chalet Gondola Stop:
◆ **Over the Bars** (road) and **Free Wheeling** (road) back to gondola base.
◆ **Over the Bars** (road) and **Follow Me** (road) to **Paper Route** (single) and back to gondola base.
◆ **Bearing Straits** (single) and **Beach Cruiser** (single) around Red's Lake and back to gondola base.

From Summit Chalet:
◆ **Kamikaze** (road) to **Beach Cruiser** (single), around Red's Lake and back to gondola base.

Optional final ride: Downhill 15 miles on vehicle roads to Hot Creek, which is closed at sunset. Arrange for Bike Park van pick-up and return to gondola base.

▲ It is actually possible for mountain bike riders to dawdle and meander when they spot a pretty view at Red's Lake.

▲ Single-track bike trails seldom have space for passing, but there is seldom a need to pass on the 75 miles of trails.

▲ Service roads (used by vehicles only during closed hours) provide bike trails which have plenty of room for passing.

▲ Hot Creek bathers tend to congregate where geothermal water from creekbed vents warm up the melted snow water.

Soak and Sleep

Hot Creek (open sunrise to sunset): A unique geothermal area where scalding mineral water bubbles up into a snow-runoff creek, resulting in water temperatures tolerable to humans. Bathing suits are required. Open from sunrise to sunset. Directions: From the town of Mammoth Lakes, drive east to US 395 and turn right (south) to the second exit, which is Owens River Road; turn left (east) and follow signs four miles to Hot Creek parking area.

Pulkey's Pool (near Hot Creek): See description and directions on Soak and Sleep page of Red's Meadow - Devil's Postpile section.

▲ Prudent parents carry curious children through the swirling water but don't let them walk near the scalding vents.

▲ The bar in this famous lodge has a big window facing the mountain, featuring skiers in winter and bikers in summer.

▼ For registered guests, three indoor hydropools are available to soak out the kinks of an active day on the slopes.

Mammoth Mountain Inn: (619) 934-0606. P.O. Box 353, Mammoth Lakes, CA 93546. Across the street from Bike Park office and gondola base. Hundreds of rooms, bar, restaurant, hydropools. Bike adventure/lodging packages available.

Forest Creek Condominiums: (619) 934-8644. In the town of Mammoth Lakes. Every unit has a kitchen and private solarium spa.

Mammoth Mountain RV Park: (619) 934-3822.
P.O. Box 288, Mammoth Lakes, CA 93546. In the town of Mammoth Lakes. Offers 138 spaces with hookups. Communal indoor swimming pool and hydropool.

National Forest Campground (Shady Rest): (619) 934-3822. Near the National Forest Visitor Center in the town of Mammoth Lakes. All camping spaces are first-come, first-served.

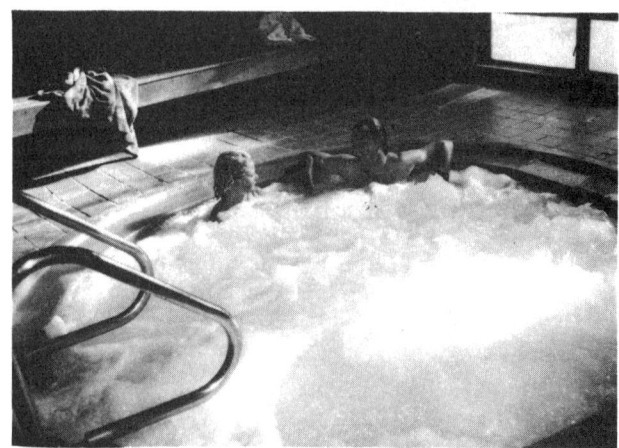

RED'S MEADOW - DEVIL'S POSTPILE

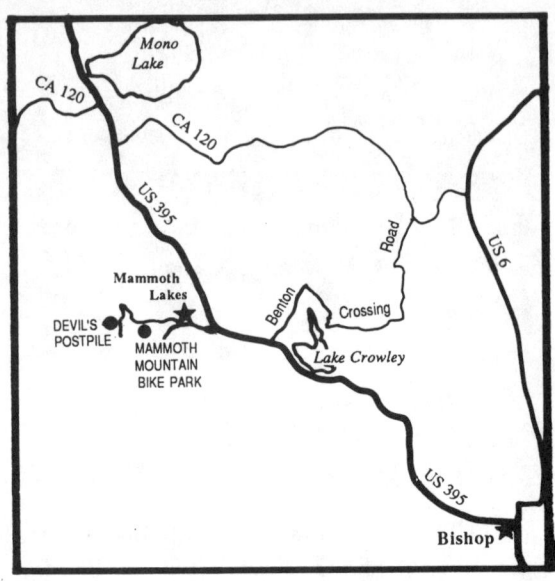

Location Overview

This spectacular eastern Sierra alpine valley in Inyo National Forest has it all: hot spring, river, waterfalls, lakes, forests, trails, and unique geological features. To reduce daytime vehicle congestion during summer months, there is mandatory daytime shuttle bus service along the floor of the valley and connecting to parking areas at nearby Mammoth Mountain Inn. Elevation 7,500 to 8,500 feet.

The principal activities are hiking, fishing, and paddle-boating on lakes. Bicycles are not permitted on trails; horses and dogs on leashes are permitted.

The valley contains several National Forest campgrounds with spaces available on a first-come, first-served basis. It is 12 miles to a fully-equipped RV park in the town of Mammoth Lakes, and four miles to hotel rooms at Mammoth Mountain Inn. It is 20 miles to Mammoth-June airport and 12 miles to Centinela-Mammoth Hospital, (619) 934-3311..

Tourist Attractions

Talk to your travel agent or contact the Mammoth Lakes Visitors Bureau, P.O. Box 48, Mammoth Lakes, CA 93546, (619) 934-2712.

▲ One of the unique shuttle bus stops is at the Devil's Postpile trailhead.

Trail Maps

This section identifies only a few of the trails available and does not attempt to provide a detailed map. Therefore, you will need an official map of Inyo National Forest, and we suggest that you obtain it ahead of time by mail. Send your request with $3.00 to Mammoth Ranger District, Inyo National Forest, P.O. Box 148, Mammoth Lakes, CA 93546. Be sure to mention the Red's Meadow - Devil's Postpile valley and ask for supplementary information about your areas of special interest, such as hiking trails, campgrounds, equestrian facilities, fishing, etc. For information call (619) 934-2505.

▲ The plaque on this monument explains in detail the geological process which resulted in the Devil's Postpile.

▲ Some of the trails are located on the banks of the San Joaquin River.

Topography and History

The San Joaquin River is best known as the main stream flowing north through California's Central Valley toward San Francisco Bay. However, the middle fork of this river actually originates in a picturesque section of the Sierra Nevada lying east of Yosemite National Park and then flows south for many miles before turning west into the Central Valley. Devil's Postpile National Monument and Red's Meadow are located in the beautiful mountain valley cut by the upper San Joaquin River. The area is part of the Inyo National Forest.

For millions of years, massive natural forces have created, shaped, carved and eroded the landscape. Molten lava flowed for miles down the slopes of active volcanoes, tons of frothy molten rock (pumice) was spewed into the air, and the solidified cores of old volcanoes weathered into craggy mountain peaks. During ice ages, years of snowfall accumulated into creeping glaciers that scoured alpine valleys down to bedrock. Recent centuries of moderate weather have formed fertile meadows and nurtured the growth of large forests, but less extreme levels of volcanic activity and earthquakes have continued right up to the present time. Red's Meadow Hot Spring is a reminder that the earth's crust floats on a potentially active reservoir of molten rock.

Approximately 100,000 years ago, basalt lava erupted from a vent in the valley, filling it to a depth of 400 feet. Surface cracks formed when tensions caused by the shrinking of the cooling lava were greater than the strength of the lava itself. Each crack branched when it reached a critical length and, together with other cracks, formed a pattern that gradually deepened to produce long basalt columns first called the Devil's Woodpile. These irregular polygons are 10 to 30 inches in diameter and stand as high as 60 feet. These remarkably smooth columns were made visible during the last ice age when glacial action scoured off the tops and one side of the basaltic mass. President Taft designated the area as the Devil's Postpile National Monument on July 6, 1911.

After ice-age glaciers gouged a hollow in the granite base of the valley and then melted away, the water of Sotcher Lake filled the resulting depression. More recent natural forces have also had an effect on this lake. Massive avalanches have roared down the adjoining mountain slopes and into and across the lake. Beavers have built a dam across the lake outlet, raising the water level several feet and drowning a stand of lodgepole pines along the northern edge.

There is only one access road into the valley via a narrow winding road through Minaret Pass, 12 miles west of the town of Mammoth Lakes. The public popularity of this valley attracted an ever-increasing number of visitors, vehicles, and gravel-road dust until 1979, when the Forest Service paved the road and initiated a mandatory day-time shuttle service during summer months. The buses run from Mammoth Mountain Inn, where there is unlimited parking, through Minaret Pass and along the full length of the road on the floor of the valley. A wide variety of short and long trails branch off from the various bus stops.

Available Activities

Your day-trip plans should be adjusted to fit current weather conditions and the physical abilities of the individuals in your group. Discuss them with a ranger when you arrive, in case one or more of the suggested activities should be replaced for your comfort and convenience.

Things to bring: sturdy walking shoes, layered clothing, sunscreen, insect repellant, first aid kit, water, lunch, camera, towel if you plan to use hot shower..

The surfaces of all suggested trails are Class 1, which means there are no irregularities higher than a standard stair step (nine inches).

This location is much too large to be fully explored in one day. The following suggested day trip program, keyed to shuttle bus stops, will provide examples of several different environments:

Devil's Postpile Bus Stop to Minaret Falls: 2.0 miles round trip. 100-foot elevation change. Easy walking.

Devil's Postpile Bus Stop to Rainbow Falls Bus Stop: 1.5 miles. 100-foot elevation change. This popular trail passes the famous Devil's Postpile.

▲ Energetic visitors can follow a side trail which leads them around and to the top of this spectacular formation.

▲ Foot-weary hikers use rustic benches to admire the Devil's Postpile in comfort.

◄ Throughout this valley the trails are well-marked and well-maintained.

105 RED'S MEADOW - DEVIL'S POSTPILE

▲ Beautiful Sotcher Lake is only 50 yards away from this shuttle bus stop.

▶ Printed guides to the nature trail are dispensed from a box located next to this descriptive map display board.

▼ These anglers increase their enjoyment of the lake by relaxing in lounge chairs while waiting for the fish to bite.

Sotcher Lake Bus Stop around Sotcher Lake Loop: 1.3 miles. 50-foot elevation change. Printed booklets available near the bus stop define and explain the features of this interesting and beautiful self-guided nature trail.

When beavers built this dam it raised the level of the lake and drowned some trees which used to be on the lake edge.

The white trees are a "ghost" forest of trees killed by the raised water level.

This waterfall tumbles over a unique volcanic formation that is explained in the printed nature trail guide.

Red's Meadow Campground Bus Stop to Red's Meadow Hot Spring: 0.5 mile round trip. Minor elevation change. Free hot showers fed by a geothermal spring are available in a six-room bathhouse.

▲▼ The Red's Meadow bath house is located in Red's Meadow Campground, a quarter-mile from the shuttle bus stop.

▲ The hot spring at Red's Meadow has been capped and the mineral water is piped to showers over bath house concrete tubs.

Soak and Sleep

Pulkey's Pool (near Hot Creek): A volunteer-built cement soaking pool fed by nearby hot springs and located on a barren section of BLM land, with a tradition of clothing-optional use. Directions: From the town of Mammoth Lakes, drive east to US 395 and turn right (south) to the third exit, Benton Crossing Road. Turn left (east) and immediately take note of the metal cattle guard in the road as you pass the small green church. Continue east, noting a second and third metal cattle guard. 0.4 mile beyond the third cattle guard, turn left on an unmarked dirt road that circles to the right around a meadow. Park in the large level area; follow a path and some boards across marshy areas to the pool at the crest of a hill.

Hot Creek: See description and directions on Soak and Sleep page of Mammoth Mountain Bike Park section.

Mammoth Mountain Inn: (619) 934-0606. P.O. Box 353, Mammoth Lakes, CA 93546. Main shuttle bus terminal. Across the street from main ski lifts. Hundreds of rooms, bar, restaurant, hydropools.

Forest Creek Condominiums: (619) 934-8644. In the town of Mammoth Lakes. Every unit has a kitchen and a private solarium spa.

Mammoth Mountain RV Park: (619) 934-3822.
P.O. Box 288, Mammoth Lakes, CA 93546. In the town of Mammoth Lakes. Offers 138 spaces with hookups. Communal indoor swimming pool and hydropool.

There is a National Monument campground at Devil's Postpile and five Forest Service campgrounds in the valley, with spaces available on a first-come, first served basis. Inquire at Minaret Entrance Station regarding procedure for campground registration during vehicle-restricted daytime hours.

At Pulkey's Pool volunteers installed gravity-flow pipes from a nearby hot spring and cold spring enabling soakers to control pool water temperature.

PORTOLA STATE PARK

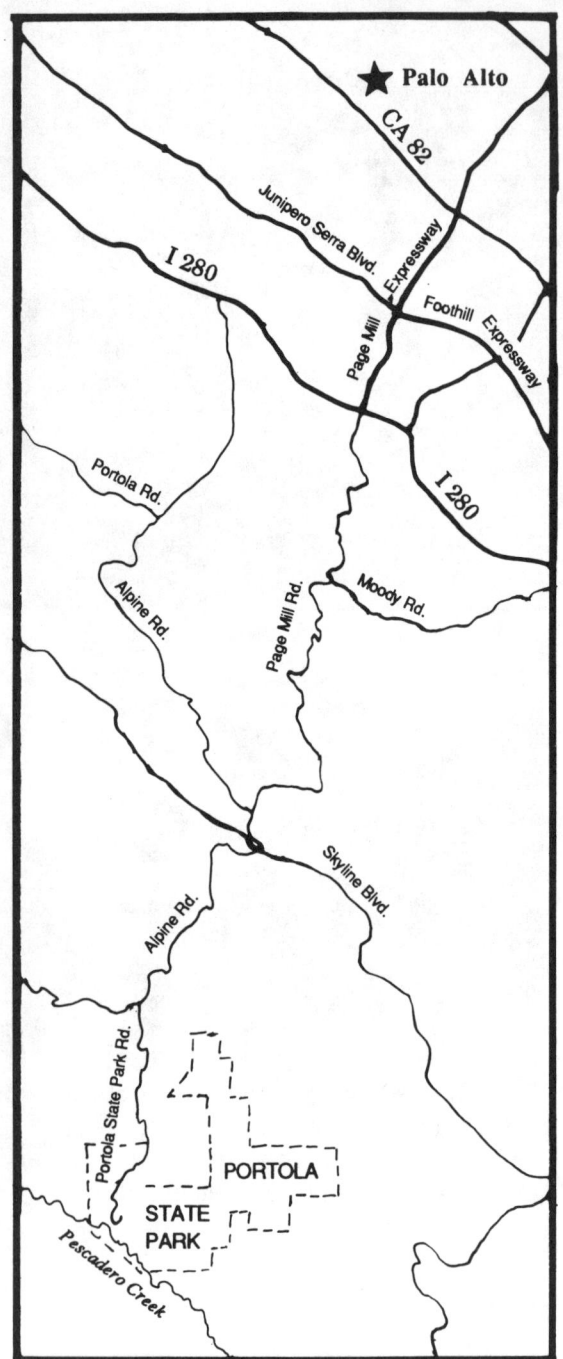

Location Overview

The park covers 2,400 acres on the west slope of the Santa Cruz Mountains, surprisingly close to Palo Alto and the Silicon Valley. All-year streams flow through lush, cool, green canyons between exposed ridges. It is often cold and damp during the rainy season from October through April. Elevation: 400 to 1,000 feet.

The available activities are primarily hiking and playing in the streams. There is a self-guided nature trail, but there are no equestrian trails and only one short road for bicycles.

Within the park there are 52 developed campsites. Motels and private hot tub rentals are available within 20 miles. It is no more that 40 miles to either the San Francisco or the San Jose International Airport, and 20 miles to Stanford Medical Center, (415) 723-5111

Tourist Attractions

Talk to your travel agent or contact the San Mateo County Chamber of Commerce, 1730 South El Camino, Suite 200, San Mateo, CA 94402, (415) 341-5679.

▲ Climbing a log over a running stream is at least twice as exciting as playing on an ordinary iron pipe jungle gym.

▲ Reclining on a log in a quiet forest is at least twice as relaxing as plowing through the crowds at a shopping mall.

Trail Maps

This section does not identify all of the activities available at this location and does not attempt to provide a detailed trail map. Therefore, you will need an official map of Portola State Park, and we recommend that you obtain it ahead of time by mail. Send your request with $1.00 to Portola State Park, Star Route 2, La Honda, CA 94020, (415) 948-9098. Be sure to ask for supplementary information about your areas of special interest, such as local natural history associations, guided nature walks, camping, hiking trails, bicycle routes, etc.

▲ The complex grain pattern of redwood burl art objects comes from the gnarled roots of fallen giants, such as this tree found along the Summit Trail.

Topography and History

In south San Mateo County, in the rugged terrain of a deep canyon between two ridges, Portola State Park offers solitude and relaxation just over the hill from San Francisco Bay. Visitors are advised to use extreme care during the last few miles of the access road where the downhill portion is narrow and steep.

The park is a natural, all-year stream basin of mixed evergreen forest featuring first-and second-growth redwoods. On exposed hillsides the redwoods give way to hardwoods and shrubs; ferns and shade-tolerant plants are found along the creeks. Pescadero Creek and Peters Creek flow along fault lines in the earth where oil seepage and marine fossil deposits hint at Portola's complex geologic history. Fishing is prohibited because salmon from the Pacific Ocean still make their annual run up Pescadero (Spanish for *fish*) Creek.

Fourteen miles of hiking trails provide opportunities to observe and enjoy this northern extremity of the Santa Cruz Mountains. In addition to the 2,400 acres at Portola, the development of adjoining Pescadero Creek County Park to the west has opened 7,000 acres of hiking and equestrian trails. Visitors are invited to explore this combined area any time of year. However, during the rainy months, footbridges over Pescadero Creek are removed, preventing access to some of the trails.

In 1769, noted Spanish explorer Don Gaspar de Portola led an expedition through present-day San Mateo County in search of Monterey Bay. Instead, he happened upon a new anchorage, the bay later named San Francisco. California's Gold Rush of 1849 began a demand for ever-increasing amounts of timber for mining operations and town building. Lumbermen became the original settlers of the Santa Cruz Mountains, cutting what seemed to be unending groves of thousand-year-old redwood trees.

The first local settler of record is Christian Iverson, a Scandanavian immigrant who worked as a pony express rider and shotgun guard. He acquired two parcels of land on Pescadero Creek in the 1860's and built a cabin that was also used by subsequent property owners and still stands today. John Hooper, a wealthy San Francisco businessman, built a two-story "summer home" on Pescadero Creek at the turn of the century. By 1924, the Islam Temple Shrine of San Francisco had purchased approximately 1,600 acres to be used as a summer retreat for members. The retreat operated until 1945, when the State of California purchased the parcel for use as a state park. Generous donations of land purchased by the Save-the-Redwoods League have increased the total area of Portola State Park to over 2,400 acres today.

▲ Small boys have a need to sit by a stream with a line on a stick, but real fishing is banned in this salmon stream.

Available Activities

Your day-trip plans should be adjusted to fit current weather conditions and the physical abilities of the individuals in your group. Discuss your plans with a ranger when you arrive in case one or more of the suggested activities should be changed for your comfort and convenience.

Things to bring: sturdy walking shoes, layered clothing, swimsuit, sunscreen, insect repellant, first aid kit, towel, water, lunch, camera.

All suggested trail surfaces are Class 1, which means that there are no irregularities higher than a standard stair step (nine inches).

This location is too large to be fully explored in one day. The following suggested day-trip program will provide examples of several different environments:

▲ When the coastal fog reaches into the redwood forest the trees seem to disappear into a magical gray sky.

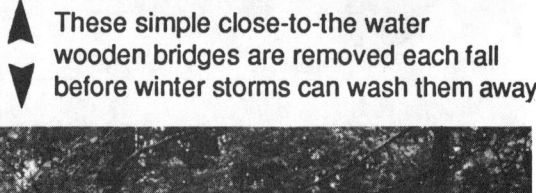

Self-Guided Nature Trail: 0.75 mile round trip. Minor elevation change. Smooth surface winds through a redwood forest adjoining Pescadero Creek; excellent for family exploration.

These simple close-to-the water wooden bridges are removed each fall before winter storms can wash them away.

Be sure to take your camera. This type of photo belongs in the family album.

Iverson Trail: 3.0 miles round trip. 50-foot elevation change. A smooth, easy-grade path follows the creek through a densely wooded area, including a side trail to Tiptoe Falls. This area takes on a very mysterious appearance when coast redwoods are shrouded in fog.

Old Tree Trail: 0.5 mile round trip. Minor elevation change. Easy walk through dense woods to a giant redwood tree.

▲ This miniature waterfall is so quiet and demure that is it aptly named "Tiptoe."

▼ The foliage is so lush that the Iverson Trail resembles a living green tunnel.

▲ It may be possible to hug one of the roots of this old tree, but there is no way for any human to hug the whole tree.

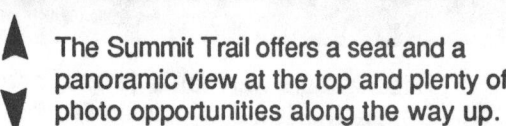

Slate Creek Trail/Summit Trail Loop: 2.0 miles. 500-foot elevation change. Smooth but sometimes steep path to a ridge-top panoramic viewpoint.

The Summit Trail offers a seat and a panoramic view at the top and plenty of photo opportunities along the way up.

Smooth well-maintained trails are part of the tradition of this state park.

▲ Large, well-shaded campsites are scattered along the banks of the creeks.

▼ Watercourse Way features tile hot tubs and Oriental decor in private spaces.

Soak and Sleep

The campground in this park has 52 developed spaces, each with table and fireplace. Restrooms with hot showers are nearby. Reservations recommended except in winter. Call MISTIX, (800) 446-7275 from within California; (619) 452-1950 from outside California.

Stanford Park Hotel Best Western: (415) 322-1234, 100 El Camino Real, Menlo Park, CA 94025. Twenty miles from park entrance. Offers 164 units, swimming pool, and hydropool.

Watercourse Way: (415) 329-8827, 165 Channing Way, Palo Alto, CA 94301. Twenty miles from park entrance. Nine individually decorated private rooms with various combinations of hot pool, cold pool, sauna, and steambath for rent by the hour. Reservations recommended.

HENRY COWELL REDWOODS STATE PARK

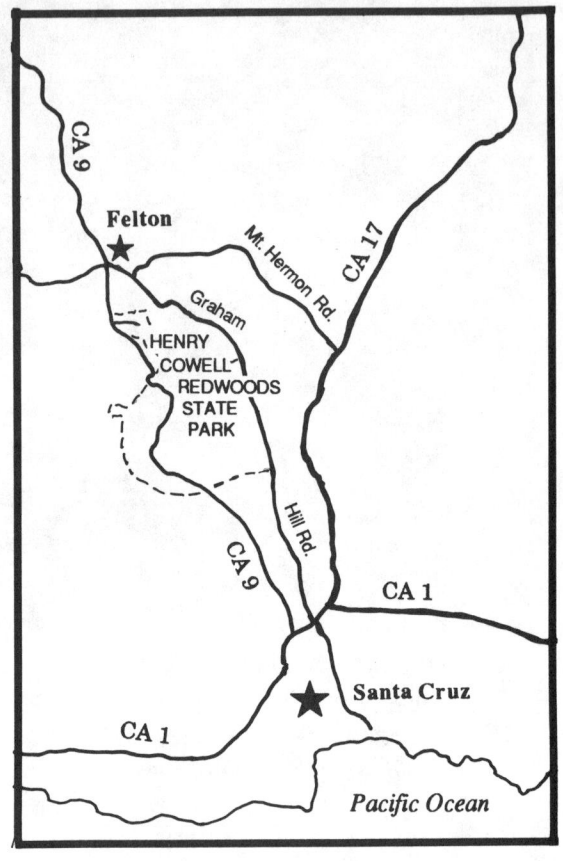

Location Overview

The park covers 1,800 acres on a south slope of the Santa Cruz mountains, straddling a section of the San Lorenzo River gorge a few miles north of Santa Cruz. There is a high, dry, chaparral-covered ridge, but most of the area is cool, tree-covered slopes, including a rare grove of giant first-growth redwood trees. It is usable year-round, but not recommended during rain. Elevation: 150 to 800 feet.

The choice of activities include river swimming, a nature trail, hiking trails, equestrian trails, and bicycle trails. The Redwood Loop Trail is handicapped-accessible. Park facilities include a Nature Center and gift shop. From a nearby station, excursion steam engine train rides are available through the woods.

The park includes a large campground and a picnic area, but day use is permitted only from 6 am to sunset. It is one mile to a motel or RV park; six miles to the hot tubs; ten miles to Dominican Santa Cruz Hospital, (408) 462-7700; and thirty miles to San Jose International Airport.

▶ An authentic steam engine pulls the sightseeing train through the redwoods.

Tourist Attractions

Talk to your travel agent or contact the Santa Cruz County Conference and Visitors Council, 701 Front Street, Santa Cruz, CA 95060, (408) 425-1234.

▲ A rare grove of giant first-growth coast redwood trees is a feature of this park.
▼ There is also a wide variety of lush foliage along the River Trail.

▲ The park includes land on both sides of the San Lorenzo River, an excellent all-year stream for family recreation.

Trail Maps

This section identifies only a few of the activities available and does not attempt to provide a detailed trail map. Therefore, you will need an official map of Henry Cowell Redwoods State Park. Send your request with $1.00 to Santa Cruz Mountains Natural History Association, 525 Big Trees Park Road, Felton, CA 95018, (408) 335-3174. Be sure to ask for supplementary information about your areas of special interest, such as local natural history associations, guided nature walks, camping, hiking trails, equestrian facilities, bicycle routes, etc.

Topography and History

This small portion of the San Lorenzo Valley contains a remarkable diversity of environment: huge venerable redwoods, lush stream canyons, open sunny meadows, pine and oak forests, and high dry chaparral ridges. Wildlife is plentiful, ranging from the commonly seen jays and squirrels to the more elusive owls and bobcats.

During prehistoric times when dinosaurs roamed the earth, redwoods were widespread over much of the northern hemisphere. Over millennia, climatic change reduced the redwood's habitat. Today these tallest trees in the world are found only along a 450-mile corridor stretching from the bottom of Oregon to the southern limits of Monterey County. Even within this range, redwoods are restricted to moist, fog-shrouded stream canyons within 30 miles of the sea.

The Ohlone Indians lived here in quiet harmony with their surroundings for many thousands of years. The Spanish and Mexican periods left their marks on the land, as did American pioneers such as Henry Cowell, who moved to the Santa Cruz area in 1865 after making his fortune in San Francisco. By 1886, his extensive land holdings totaled 6,500 acres, including several limekiln production sites, and a ranch that is now occupied by the University of California campus.

In 1875, an eight-mile stretch of railroad was constructed from the town of Felton to Santa Cruz to facilitate the transport of lumber from the mountains to the coast for shipping. Soon this section was connected to a new line that climbed over the summit from San Jose. In addition to freight, the trains began to bring in thousands of tourists who were eager to see Santa Cruz's famous big trees and enjoy nearby sandy ocean beaches.

The most impressive grove of redwoods along the rail line was owned by Joseph Welch. To meet the demands of tourists, he built a resort complete with cabins, dining hall and dance pavilion. Welch's Big Trees Resort was on the itinerary of nearly every visitor to the Santa Cruz area, including such famous dignitaries as Presidents Benjamin Harrison and Theodore Roosevelt.

▲ A redwood stump, ringed with second-growth trees, is a fine reading room.

In 1920, the Welch family sold the famous 120-acre parcel to Santa Cruz County, which operated it as Big Trees Park for the next 23 years. The county's property was nearly surrounded by acreage owned by the Cowell family. In 1953, Henry's son Samuel, seeking a suitable monument to his pioneering father, offered to give the state 1,600 acres of surrounding land provided that the county deed over its Big Trees Park. In 1954, the combined property became Henry Cowell Redwoods State Park.

Today the park is a unique combination of easy accessibility, comfortable facilities, an incomparable redwood grove, miles of hiking trails, and a beautiful boulder-strewn, all-year stream. Year-round camping is available on Graham, Hill Road, where a 112 unit campground features developed campsites with tables, fire rings, flush toilets and hot showers. The sites are suitable for tents and RVs, but there are no hook-ups.

▲
▼ Redwoods make up only one part of the forest in this large park. On the higher slopes, near the campground, oak trees arch gracefully over the trail. At the top of the ridge, scattered pine trees and chaparral line a sunny path.

Available Activities

Your day-trip plans should be adjusted to fit current weather conditions and the physical abilities of the individuals in your group. Discuss your plans with a ranger when you arrive in case one or more of the suggested activities should be changed for your comfort and convenience.

Things to bring: sturdy walking shoes, layered clothing, swimsuit, sunscreen, insect repellant, first aid kit, towel, water, lunch, camera.

Trail surfaces are classified as follows:

Class 1. Generally smooth with no irregularities higher than a standard stair step (nine inches).

Class 2. Some irregularities higher than a standard stair step, but none higher than two stair steps (18 inches).

Class 3. Some irregularities higher than 18 inches.

This location is too large to be fully explored in one day. The following suggested day-trip program will provide examples of several different environments:

River Trail and Rincon Trail to streambank: 2.6 miles round trip from the Nature Center. River Trail portion is Class 1 with 100-foot elevation change. Rincon Trail portion includes some Class 2 sections and drops steeply more than 400 feet down to the river gorge. Cathedral Redwoods, near the crest of Rincon Trail, is a peaceful site for lunch or a rest break.

Redwood Loop Trail: 0.8 miles round trip. No elevation gain. Flat, smooth surface, handicapped-accessible and suitable for wheelchairs. This is a self-guided nature trail through the famous Big Trees Grove. Request a printed brochure at the Nature Center.

▲ Rainy season run-off in the San Lorenzo River has built some small beaches along the lower section of the River Trail.

▲ Educational exhibits are located at the entrance to the Redwood Loop Trail.

▲ The smooth level paths of the Redwood Loop Trail are near the parking area and suitable for strollers and wheel chairs.

▲ This observation tower, with a panoramic view of the Santa Cruz Mountains, crowns the highest ridge in the park.

Eagle Creek Trail and Pine Trail to Observation Deck: 3.0 miles round trip from Nature Center. 500-foot elevation change. Class 1 and Class 2 sections with some steep grades and unshaded soft sand portions near the Observation Deck. This is also a designated equestrian trail, so be alert.

▲ Tall second-growth redwoods shade the lower portions of Eagle Creek Trail.

▲ This bridge over Eagle Creek is surrounded by the lush foliage which lines the banks of all-year streams.

▲
▼ Parents and children work together to explore rocks along the river's edge. Even if diving were permitted, none of the pools are deep enough for diving.

Garden of Eden Trail: On the west side of the river, reached from a parking area on Hwy 9, 1.3 miles south of the Park Entrance. 1.5 miles round trip from the parking area. 100-foot elevation change. Class 1 except for some Class 2 sections in last 50 yards near the river's edge. The lovely small sand beaches between large piles of boulders have a tradition of clothing-optional use.

◄ Part of the trail to Garden of Eden runs along these railroad tracks, giving visitors a chance to test their balancing skills.

Soak and Sleep

The campground in this park has its own separate entrance off of Graham Hill Road. 112 developed campsites with tables, fire rings, flush toilets and hot showers. Reservations recommended except in winter; phone MISTIX, (800) 444 PARK, in California; (619) 452-1950 from outside California.

Smithwoods RV Park: (408) 335-4321.
4770 Hwy 9, Felton, CA 95018. One mile from Park Entrance. Includes 130 spaces with hook-ups. Swimming pool.

Fernriver Resort Motel: (408) 3325-4412
5250 Hwy 9, Felton, CA 95018. One mile from Park Entrance. Mountain location with 13 rooms, each with a fireplace.

Babbling Brook Bed & Breakfast Inn: (408) 427-2437. 1025 Laurel Street, Santa Cruz, CA 95060. Six miles from Park Entrance. Offers 12 units, some with in-room hot tub and fireplace.

Holiday Inn: (408) 426-7100.
611 Ocean Street, Santa Cruz, CA 95060. Six miles from Park Entrance. Includes 54 units, some with in-room hot tub. Restaurant on premises.

Kiva Retreat: (408) 429-1142.
702 Water Street, Santa Cruz, CA 95060. Six miles from Park Entrance. Two large hot tubs in communal clothing-optional garden. Private hot tub and massage are available by appointment.

▲ Camping sites within the park are located on a dry oak-shaded plateau about a mile from the river.

▲ A private hot pool can be reserved, but this garden-area communal pool at Kiva Retreat is available at any time.

THE FOREST OF NISENE MARKS STATE PARK

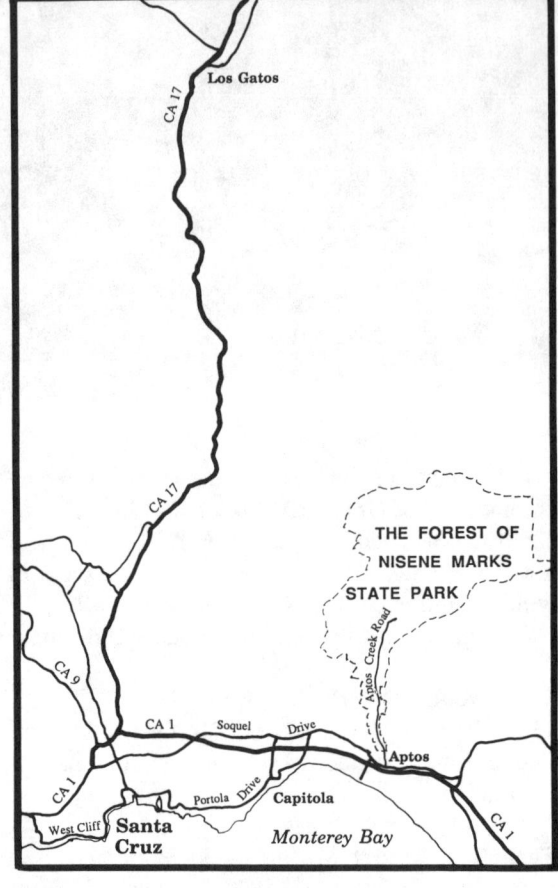

Location Overview

The park covers 10,000 acres on the southwest slope of the Santa Cruz Mountains, stretching from hot exposed ridges to lush green, cool canyons with all-year streams in the lower reaches. It is enjoyable year-round but not recommended during rain. Elevation: 100 to 2,600 feet.

The activities are primarily hiking and playing in the streams. There are no visitor centers and no self-guided nature trails. Bicycles are permitted only on the road, and equestrian use is limited to the lower portion of the park.

Within the state park there are no vehicle campgrounds, and overnight parking is prohibited. Campgrounds, RV parks, motels and rental hot tubs are available within ten miles. It is six miles to Dominican Santa Cruz Hospital, (408) 462-7700, and 35 miles to the San Jose International Airport.

Tourist Attractions

Talk to your travel agent or contact the Santa Cruz County Conference and Visitors Council, 701 Front Street, Santa Cruz, CA 95060, (408) 425-1234.

▲ Along the single access road into this park, trail information is abundant.

▲ This is the intersection of Aptos Creek Road and Soquel Drive in Aptos.

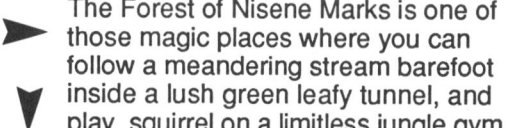

► The Forest of Nisene Marks is one of those magic places where you can follow a meandering stream barefoot inside a lush green leafy tunnel, and
▼ play squirrel on a limitless jungle gym.

Trail Maps

This section identifies only a few of the activities available and does not attempt to provide a detailed trail map. Therefore, you will need an official map of The Forest of Nisene Marks State Park, and we recommend that you obtain it ahead of time by mail. Send your request with $1.00 to The Forest of Nisene Marks State Park, 525 North Big Trees Park Road, Felton, CA 95018, (408) 335-4598. Be sure to ask for supplementary information about your areas of special interest such as local natural history associations, guided nature walks, camping, hiking trails, equestrian facilities, bicycle routes, etc.

Topography and History

Some of the Santa Cruz Mountains State Parks contain large groves of first-growth redwood trees because courageous people were willing to intervene and save the trees before they were cut down. Henry Cowell State Park and Big Basin State Park are monuments to such courage and foresight. On the other hand, The Forest of Nisene Marks State Park is on land that was clear-cut during a forty-year logging frenzy (1883-1923). When the loggers left Aptos Canyon, the forest began to heal itself and now the scars grow fainter with each passing year. The Forest of Nisene Marks is a tribute to forest regeneration and to the future - it is a forest in a state of becoming.

The forest's land is a maze of ridges and canyons formed by the twisting and contorting of the earth due to faults that run diagonally across the park. The epicenter of the 1989 Loma Prieta earthquake has been located in the park - actually 12 miles straight down in the earth's crust under the park. There is a sign identifying the general location, but there is no visible evidence of quake damage, such as surface faulting.

The park contains the climatic extremes of hot, exposed ridge tops and dark, cool canyons. Before the logging era, the canyon's vegetation zones varied with the altitude in a clearly defined manner. The creekside riparian plant community (big leaf maples, red alder) changed to a redwood forest on the lower canyon walls. Set apart above the redwood forest was a mixed evergreen forest (madrone, douglas fir, tan oak), which at 1,800 feet gave way to a chaparral community (manzanita, buck brush, knobcone pine). The logger's clear-cutting blurred the vegetation zones. Until the second-growth redwoods regain their supremacy in the canyon's lower reaches, there will be an intermingling of riparian and evergreen forest.

▲ This sign, marking the earthquake epicenter area, is on an easy trail.

▼ The turn-of-the-century logging frenzy took some huge first-growth trees, leaving mammoth stumps to burn and rot away. The surrounding second-growth redwood trees have sprouted from the roots of this now-hollow giant.

In 1844, the canyon was part of the Soquel Augmentation Mexican land grant given to Martina Castro. In 1883, the Castro family sold the property to the Loma Prieta Lumber Company, a Watsonville-based firm that joined forces with the Southern Pacific Railroad Company. Enormous financial and technological resources were focused on the redwood-filled canyon, and a massive broad gauge railroad was forced through the funnel mouth to a point seven miles from the Southern Pacific tracks in Aptos.

The lumber company's 9,600 acres were purchased in the 1950s by the Marks, a family of Danish ancestry active in Salinas Valley farming. In 1963, Herman, Agnes and Andrew Marks, with assistance from the Nature Conservancy, donated the property to the State of California in memory of their mother, Nisene Marks. The donation was made with the stipulation that the property be left undeveloped so that the natural process of restoration might continue. Since 1963, with help from the Save-the-Redwoods League, new properties have been purchased downstream from the original Marks donation. Under the stewardship of the State of California, the process of natural restoration continues.

The natural inaccessibility of the canyons was brought into dramatic focus during the winter storms of 1982 and 1983; creeks raged through the canyons, scouring creek bottoms and tossing logs about like tinker toys. Many of the hiking trails that had been placed atop hundred-year-old railroad grades were washed away; trestles which had witnessed a century of storms vanished without a trace. Some of the trails on the Bridge Creek and West Ridge sides of the park were restored by volunteer workers and the California Youth Conservation Corps, but it will be many years before the hiking trail system is once again extended into the farthest reaches of Aptos Creek Canyon.

▲ An unknown volunteer installed this rope on a creekside tree. The young-at-heart are always tempted to make at least one Tarzan swing over the water.

Available Activities

Your day-trip plans should be adjusted to fit current weather conditions and the physical abilities of the individuals in your group. Discuss your plans with a ranger when you arrive, in case one or more of the suggested activities should be changed for your comfort and convenience.

Things to bring: sturdy walking shoes, layered clothing, swimsuit, sunscreen, insect repellant, first aid kit, towel, water, lunch, camera.

Trail surfaces are classed as follows:

Class 1. Generally smooth with no irregularities higher than a standard stair step (nine inches).

Class 2. Some irregularities higher than a standard stair step, but none higher than two stair steps (18 inches).

Class 3. Some irregularities higher than 18 inches.

This location is much too large to be fully explored in one day. The following suggested day-trip program will provide examples of several different environments:

Aptos Creek Fire Road to Earthquake Epicenter Area: 3.0 miles round trip. 200-foot elevation change. Class 1 surface except for one creek crossing on stepping stones, which can be avoided by a short detour via the Loma Prieta Grade Trail and Mill Pond Trail. This is a wide, well-shaded, easy-slope route along the edge of Aptos Creek.

▲
▼
One step at a time on the rocks is the old-fashioned way to cross a creek. The rest of the Aptos Creek Fire Road is a gentle grade wide enough for both bicycles and hikers.

▲ Some of the side trails over smaller creeks use a single log bridge instead of a string of stepping-stones.

Porter Trail/Access Road Loop: 1.2 miles. 200-foot elevation change. A winding, occasionally steep path through groves of second-growth redwoods, with creekside picnic tables at Porter Family Picnic Area.

Terrace Trail Loop: 1.5 miles. 100-foot elevation change. Mostly Class 1 surface with a few Class 2 stretches. A shady, sometimes uneven path along both sides of the lower reaches of Aptos Creek.

▲ The Porter Trail creek crossing at the beautiful Porter Family Picnic Area is an ideal place for parents to join their children in exploring the streambed.

▲ For school-age children, large shallow sandy-bottom pools are more fun than a wind-up toy, while parents can relax in the shade with the small fry.

Alternate Day-Trip Program:

Loop Route via Loma Prieta Grade Trail to Maple Falls and return via Bridge Creek Trail: 8.0 miles. 500-foot elevation change. Class 1 surface while on old railroad grades, degenerating to a strenuous Class 3 non-trail for the last 3/4 mile to Maple Falls. Bridge Creek Historic Site is ideal for a lunch break and a stretched-out rest.

There is no maintatined trail in the canyon which leads to Maple Falls, so expect to do a lot of tree-walking and rock-hopping to reach the falls.

Beautiful Maple Falls scatters a most welcome cooling mist on hot hikers.

▲ Rest stops for tired legs are wherever and whenever you decide to sit down.

▼ In the hot tub at days end, your whole body gets a reward for enabling you to be in nature and be a part of nature.

Soak and Sleep

Within the state park there are no vehicle campgrounds, and overnight parking is prohibited.

New Brighton Beach State Park: (408) 475-4850. Three miles from Nisene Marks entrance. Offers 115 developed campsites, including 15 tent sites, some directly above the beach. Reservations recommended except in winter; phone MISTIX (800) 444 PARK, in California; (619) 452-1950 from outside California.

KOA Kampgrounds of America: (408) 722-0552. 1186 San Andreas Road, Watsonville, CA 95076. Ten miles from Nisene Marks entrance. Has 223 RV sites, 23 tent sites, 20 camping cabins, swimming pool, hydropool. Reservations with deposits required.

Seacliff Inn: (408) 688-7300.
7500 Old Dominion Way, Aptos, CA 05003. Two miles from Nisene Marks entrance. 140 units, swimming pool and hydropool, and some luxury units with private hydropools.

Mangels House: (408) 688-7982.
570 Aptos Creek Road, Aptos, CA 95001. Victorian bed and breakfast inn along the road to Nisene Marks State Park.

Heartwood Spa: (408) 462-2192.
3150A Mission Drive, Santa Cruz, CA 95065. Five miles from Nisene Marks entrance. Day use only. Large hot tub in communal clothing-optional garden. Private hot tub and massage available by appointment.

POINT LOBOS STATE RESERVE

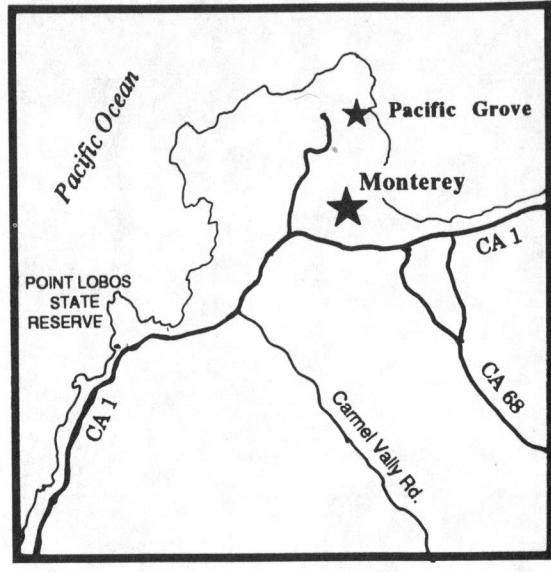

Tourist Attractions
Talk to your travel agent or contact the Monterey Visitor Information Center, Alvarado Street, Monterey, CA 93940, (408) 649-1770.

Location Overview
A landscape artist called this "the greatest meeting of land and water in the world." It is 554 acres of bold headlands, irregular coves, and rolling meadows. The climate is generally moderate, with morning fog and afternoon sun, but winter weather can be harsh. Some trails and vista points are handicapped-accessible. Elevation: sea level.

The activity choices include walking on an extensive trail system, tidepool exploring on designated beaches, and scuba diving at Whaler's Cove. No fires, fishing, horses, bicycles or dogs are allowed.

Attendance is limited to 450 persons, so come early on summer weekends or you may have to wait in line for someone else to leave. There are no campgrounds or overnight parking. It is 20 miles to a state campground; four miles to a motel and nine miles to the hot tubs; four miles to Community Hospital, (408) 649-0770; and ten miles to Monterey Peninsula Airport.

 Ocean views like this caused some of the land to be sold for residential lots back in the 1800s, but the lots were eventually repurchased and included in the property donated to the state.

▲▼ The sky, clouds, colorful foliage, white breakers, and ceaseless motion of the ocean have challenged the ability of landscape artists for decades.

Trail Maps

This section identifies only a few of the activities available and does not attempt to provide a detailed trail map. Therefore, you will need an official map of Point Lobos State Reserve, and we recommend that you obtain it ahead of time by mail. Send your request with $1.00 to Point Lobos State Reserve, Route 1, Box 62, Carmel, CA 93923, (408) 624-4909. Be sure to ask for supplementary information about your areas of special interest, such as local natural history associations, guided nature walks, camping, hiking trails, etc.

See page 190

▲▼ The restless ocean breaks constantly over the jagged rocks at South Point while harbor seals take it easy on the protected rocks within Moss Cove.

Topography and History

The Point Lobos landscape was produced over millions of years through interaction between land and sea. Rocks formed below the surface were uplifted, exposed and then shaped by waves and weather into a variety of forms. Sands and gravels eroded from these rocks by a changing sea level have been deposited into an array of beaches and terraces.

Mounds of shell fragments and the presence of mortars hollowed out of bedrock indicate that Indians gathered and prepared food here. A permanent settlement was never established because fresh water disappeared during the summer and fall.

After the arrival of Europeans in 1769, Point Lobos became at various times a pasture for livestock, the site of a whaling station, an abalone cannery, and a shipping point for coal mined nearby. A portion was even subdivided into residential lots. In the early days, ownership of the land changed frequently - once supposedly during a card game.

By 1898, Point Lobos had been acquired by an owner whose foresight led to its protection. A. M. Allan bought a parcel that included portions of Point Lobos and then began to buy back the residential lots. With funds from the Save-the-Redwoods League, encouragement from an aroused public, and the gift of the Cypress Grove as a memorial dedicated to Allan and his wife, Point Lobos became part of the new state park system in 1933. Additions since then have expanded the Reserve to 554 acres. In 1960, 750 submerged acres were added, creating the first underwater reserve in the nation. This portion was designated an Ecological Reserve in 1973.

The natural processes occurring at Point Lobos are generally left undisturbed. Management does, however, include the use of fire, which has always been a natural feature of the environment. Evidence of controlled burns may be visible. Roads and signs have been kept to a minimum, and strict rules have been enacted to protect the area for future generations.

Vegetation ranges from the gnarled Monterey Cypress and tall Monterey Pines, through head-high stands of evergreen shrubs, to grassy meadows sprinkled with delicate wildflowers. Below the cliffs, in and beyond the surf, there is an underwater world of marine algae and floating kelp canopies.

The sea is also home to Gray Whales, Southern Sea Otters, Harbor Seals and California Sea Lions. The noisy barking of the sea lions inspired the earlier Spanish name of "Punta De Los Lobos Marinos," which translates to "Point of the Sea Wolves."

The Reserve's bountiful natural resources attract birds of the forest, meadow, shore and sea. Many birds, such as the slate-backed Western Gull, are here all year, while others are winter or summer visitors, and some stop only briefly during migration.

The purpose of a State Reserve is to preserve native ecological associations, unique animal and plant life, geological features and scenic qualities in an undisturbed condition. Public enjoyment and education must be conducted in a manner consistent with the preservation of natural features. Therefore, the Reserve is open only for day use, and entry at any one time is limited to a carrying capacity of 450 persons.

▲ This natural environment at North Point has the appearance of being a movie studio set for a romantic film.

▲ Guide wires have been installed to keep visitors on the path near the cliffs.

▲ At Whaler's Cove divers can explore the nation's first underwater reserve.

Available Activities

Your day-trip plans should be adjusted to fit current weather conditions and the physical abilities of the individuals in your group. Discuss your plans with a park ranger when you arrive in case one or more of the suggested activities should be changed for your comfort or convenience.

Things to bring: sturdy walking shoes, layered clothing, sunscreen, insect repellant, first aid kit, lunch, camera.

All trail surfaces are Class 1, which means no irregularities higher than a standard stair step (nine inches). Some trails to vista points are wheelchair-accessible from nearby parking lots or roadside pullouts.

The area is too large to be fully explored in one day. The following suggested day-trip program will provide examples of several different environments:

Granite Point/Moss Cove Trails: 1.9 miles round trip from Whaler's Cottage parking lot, which has a picnic area with tables. No elevation change. Smooth easy walk. Sea otters and harbor seals can usually be seen in Whaler's Cove, and Carmel is visible in the scenic vistas to the north.

Bird Island Trail: 0.8 miles round trip from Bird Island parking lot, which has a picnic area with tables. Small elevation change. There are stair steps at the beginning of the trail and more steps leading down to the beach. During spring and summer months, Bird Island does indeed become a very large bird colony.

Alternate Day-Trip Program:

Complete Reserve Perimeter Loop: 6.0 miles, including local loops. Minor elevation change. Generally smooth with some steps and some uneven rocky areas. Start at, and return to the Entrance Ranger Station.

▼ Harbor seals, such as these in Moss Cove, are part of the natural environment protected by this reserve.

▲ This view from Moss Cove Trail is so pleasing that these visitors chose to relax and soak it in for a while.

▲ This unusual natural jungle gym grows in the middle of a picnic area at the Bird Island parking area and trailhead.

Cypress Grove Loop Trail: 0.8 miles round trip from parking lot at Information Station. No elevation change. Easy trail, slightly uneven in rocky areas. This westernmost headland offers a quiet memorial grove and scenic ocean views populated with sea lions and sea otters.

▲ At South Point the Cypress Trail leads over some rocky areas, including some steps cut directly into the stone.

▲ Allan Memorial Grove, on the Cypress Trail, honors the foresighted couple who helped establish this state reserve.

▲ At South Point on the Cypress Trail nature has even provided seating accommodations for visitors who want to stop and admire the beautiful view.

Motel accommodations are available five miles away in Carmel, which is visible in the left background of this photo.

Soak and Sleep

Within this Reserve there are no campgrounds, and overnight parking is prohibited.

Pfeifer Big Sur State Park: (408) 667-2315. Twenty miles from Reserve. Offers 217 developed sites, some rental cabins. Reservations recommended except in winter; phone MISTIX (800) 444-PARK, in California; (619) 452-1950 from outside California.

Best Western Carmel Mission Inn: (408) 624-1841. 3665 Rio Road, Carmel, CA 93922. Five miles from Reserve. Includes 165 units, swimming pool, and hydropool.

Carmel Highlands Inn: (408) 624-3801. P.O. Box 1700, Carmel, CA 93921. Five miles from Reserve. Includes 142 units, swimming pool and hydropool, and some luxury suites with private hydropools.

Different Soaks: (408) 646-8293. 1157 Forest Avenue, Pacific Grove, CA 93950. Nine miles from Reserve. Day use only. Five private-space hot tubs for rent by the hour. One of the tubs is large enough for ten people, and rooms can be combined for larger groups.

Four miles beyond Carmel is Pacific Grove, the location of rental hot tubs.

SAND DOLLAR BEACH

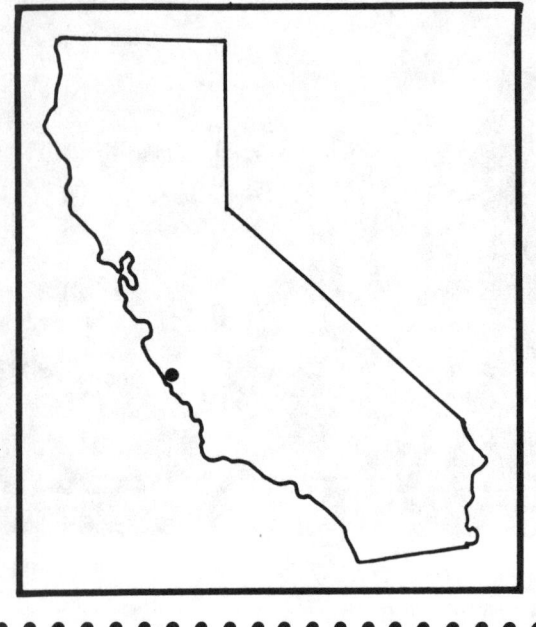

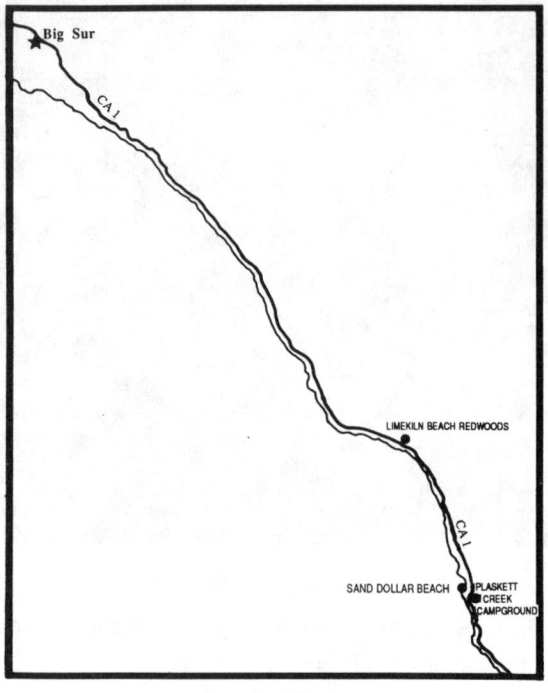

Tourist Attractions

Talk to your travel agent or contact the Monterey Peninsula Chamber of Commerce and Visitors & Convention Bureau, P.O. Box 1770, Monterey, CA 93942, (408) 648-5350.

Trail Maps

This day-trip program does not include any hiking trails, but we recommend that you obtain a Los Padres National Forest map ahead of time by mail to more easily locate the described points of interest. Send your request with $2.00 to USDA Forest Service, Monterey Ranger District, 406 South Mildred Street, King City, CA 93930, (408) 385-5434.

Location Overview

The rugged Big Sur coast is mostly jagged rocks and thundering waves, but this half-mile of gently sloping beach in Los Padres National Forest is ideal for relaxed enjoyment during summer months. It is so big and so far from major population centers that it is never crowded, even on holiday week-ends. However, ideal conditions are sometimes reduced by fog or wind. Elevation: 10 feet.

All types of surf and beach activities are available, including watching hang gliders soar from the cliffs.

The beach is never crowded, but all forms of overnight accommodations are scarce in this area. A National Forest campground is 500 yards away, a commercial campground is available within 7 miles, and a motel is within 15 miles. It is 23 miles to Esalen Institute, which occasionally has overnight accommodations with hot pool use available on short notice. It is 85 miles to commercial hot pools.

▲ Surrounding the parking lot on top of the cliff is a wide lawn with many trees, picnic tables, and fire pits.

▼ Halfway down the trail to the beach is an observation deck with display boards explaining the geology of the area.

143 SAND DOLLAR BEACH

Topography and History

The jagged Big Sur coast has the look of a classic encounter between an irresistible force (the ocean) and an immovable object (the land). Actually, that land began millions of years ago as layers of sediment on the ocean floor, covered over with many layers of lava flow. As the Pacific plate began to push under the North American plate, the whole mass was fractured and thrust up above the sea, becoming what is known as the Santa Lucia mountains. Now the waves and currents of the Pacific seem intent on trying to reclaim, one rock at a time, that which once belonged beneath the sea.

The Spanish explorers chose not to land on the inhospitable coast, simply naming it *el pais grande del sur*, "the big country to the south," and sailing on to find better harbors. The growth of Monterey and San Francisco during the 1800s created a demand for lumber, tanbark and lime, which were found along many of the Big Sur creeks. Landings sprang up at the creek mouths to meet this demand, and shipping continued until the timber and kiln firewood supplies were exhausted.

During the 1800s a primitive, often-impassable wagon road was pushed slowly south along the coast from Monterey by the early settlers in the area. It was not until 1897 that Dr. John Roberts proposed a public road from Monterey to San Luis Obispo. He walked the entire distance, mapping the contours of the land as the basis for planning the construction. In 1915 the California legislature approved the initial funds, but it was not until 1937 that the frustrating job of building Hwy 1 was completed.

Big Sur coastal weather is generally mild, often with some morning fog and afternoon wind. Daytime high temperatures are usually in the 50s in the winter and in the 60s during the summer. January and February are the wettest months, with some storm fronts coming through in late fall and early spring.

▲ Sturdy stair steps with hand rails have been constructed to provide visitors with a safe route down to beach level.

▲ A young driver gets advice on how to drive a dump truck through deep sand.

▲ There is plenty of room on this huge beach for visitors to erect volleyball nets without crowding anyone else.

▼ There is also plenty of room for paddleball games, and for young athletes to more or less patiently wait their turn.

Centuries of stream-flow down the west slope of the mountains has carved out rocky canyons that discharge sparkling fresh water directly into rocky coves. About 40 miles south of the Big Sur lighthouse, a narrow coastal mesa separates the mountains from the sea. For several miles along Hwy 1 there are picturesque spots below the cliffs where wind, tides and current have accumulated enough sand to create beaches. Sand Dollar Beach is the largest, and the only one with a flight of stairs to provide safe access to surf level. Near the top of the stairs is a large parking lot surrounded by a grassy, tree-shaded picnic area, complete with tables, water faucets, elevated fire pits and restrooms.

Jade Cove is located about a mile south of Sand Dollar Beach. Valuable and semi-valuable forms of jade have been found in this series of coves during the last two centuries, including a 4.5-ton piece worth more than $175,000, retrieved from under the water in 1971. The wave-tossed rocks in the coves are regularly combed by experienced jade hunters, so don't build unrealistic expectations about finding jade of your own.

Available Activities

Your day-trip plans should be adjusted to fit current weather conditions and the physical abilities of the individuals in your group. The suggested day trip program at this location is primarily geared to the surf and sand opportunities provided by Sand Dollar Beach and require nothing more strenuous than climbing the access stairs. The optional extra activity, Jade Cove, should be discused with the ranger at nearby Pacific Valley Guard Station (806) 927-4211.

Things to bring to the beach: Blanket or tarp, suitable footwear, layered clothing, swimsuit, towel, sunscreen, insect repellant, first aid kit, water, camera, frisbee, inner tube, inflatable mattress.

Sand Dollar Beach and Picnic Area: Leave lunch in the car and take the stairs down to the beach. Pick a place to spread the blanket and then explore the length of the beach. Return to the picnic area for lunch, then back to the beach for surf play, frisbee throwing, volleyball watching, etc.

This independent girl loves to run around and challenge the waves by herself, but mama can lend a hand, temporarily, when the big waves come.

▲ This gently sloping beach is ideal for walking an inflatable raft out through several waves and then letting the surf propel it back to the shallows.

▲ This sign on the trail to Jade Cove defines the limits within which visitors may search for and remove minerals.

▼ This is the good portion of the trail down the cliff to the beach at Jade Cove. Lower portions are badly eroded.

Jade Cove (optional extra): About one mile south of Sand Dollar Beach on Hwy 1, look on the right side for a small brown "Jade Cove" sign at a large pull-off area. The partially washed-out trail down the face of the 200-foot cliff has several Class 3 sections.

Limekiln Beach Redwoods (optional extra): This commercial campground has creekside campsites and a beautiful half-mile creekside walk through giant redwoods and verdant ferns. An additional 500-yard scramble over rocks and logs will take you to a spectacular waterfall. Occasionally, when parking space is filled, this place is closed to day use, so telephone ahead on busy weekends.

Soak and Sleep

A National Forest campground (Plaskett Creek) is across Hwy 1 from the Sand Dollar Beach parking area. The 36 campsites are available on a first-come/first-served basis.

Limekiln Beach Redwoods: (408) 667-2403.
Hwy 1, Big Sur, CA 93920. Seven miles from Sand Dollar Beach. Offers 60 camping spaces, hot showers.

Lucia Lodge: (408) 667-2391.
Hwy 1, Big Sur, CA 93920. Fifteen miles from Sand Dollar Beach. Offers 10 picturesque cabins on a cliff overlooking the ocean.

Esalen Institute: (408) 667-3000.
Hwy 1, Big Sur, CA 93920. Twenty three miles from Sand Dollar Beach. Esalen is a pioneer in the growth-center movement, specializing in residential programs that focus on education, philosophy and the physical and behavioral sciences. Access to the grounds is permitted only to workshop participants and people registered for room and board, which is occasionally available on short notice. Phone or write for a catalog of programs being offered; attendance is by prior registration and confirmation only. Registered guests have access to multiple mineral-water soaking tubs located on a cliff directly above the surf.

Different Soaks: (408)646-8293.
1157 Forest Avenue, Pacific Grove, CA 93950. Eighty five miles from Sand Dollar Beach. Five indoor, private-space hot tubs available for rent by the hour.

▲ A local resident shows off a piece of jade which he found during low tide in one of the little coves near Jade Cove.

▲ The large hydropool at Different Soaks has plenty of room for a whole family.

MONTANA DE ORO STATE PARK

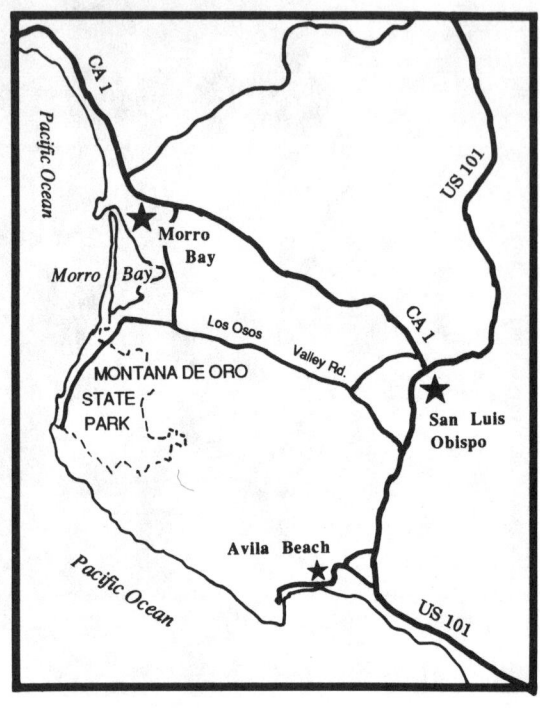

Location Overview

This 8,000 acre park south of Morro Bay includes seven miles of spectacular coastline and foothill canyons with all-year streams. Elevation: sea level to 1,500 feet.

Excellent family-oriented activities include exploring acres of safe tide pools, enjoying a shallow fresh water pond at the main beach, and sliding down the immense sand dunes. There are also miles of equestrian and bicycle trails plus a hikers-only trail in a tree-shaded canyon.

This state park includes a vehicle campground with 50 spaces and several horse camps. Motel accommodations are available within five miles, and outdoor mineral-water hot tubs for rent by the hour are available within 20 miles. It is 20 miles to the San Luis Obispo Airport and 15 miles to Sierra Vista Hospital, (805) 546-7600.

Tourist Attractions

Talk to your travel agent or contact the San Luis Obispo Chamber of Commerce, 1039 Chorro Street, San Luis Obispo, CA 93401, (805) 543-1323.

Trail Maps

This section identifies only a few of the activities available and does not attempt to provide a detailed trail map. Therefore, you will need an official map of Montana De Oro State Park, and we recommend that you obtain it ahead of time by mail. Send your request with $1.00 to Montana De Oro State Park, Los Osos, CA 93402, (805) 528-0513. Be sure to ask for supplementary information about your areas of special interest, such as local natural history associations, guided nature walks, camping, hiking trails, equestrian facilities, bicycle routes, etc.

▲ The beach at Spooner's Cove has the benefit of easy access and headlands to protect it from onshore winds.

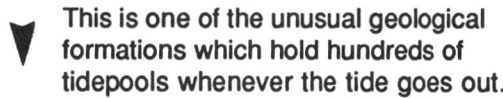
▼ This is one of the unusual geological formations which hold hundreds of tidepools whenever the tide goes out.

Topography and History

A wonderful variety of scenic, natural and recreational opportunities is available in the state parks and beaches of the Morro Bay area, located along the central California coastline, halfway between San Francisco and Los Angeles. The climate is mild in winter and cool in summer, with considerable fog and overcast. The Morro Bay Museum of Natural History offers many exhibits, films and other programs describing Native-American life in this area as well as the geology, oceanography, marine biology, botany, and zoology of the central coast region.

Montana de Oro State Park covers 8,000 acres and faces the ocean just south of Morro Bay. Its waveswept seven-mile-long shoreline is made up of large beaches along the sandspit to the north and rugged cliffs and headlands to the south. The central and southern parts of the park also feature a number of small coves with sandy beaches, the most prominent and accessible of which is Spooner's Cove. Park headquarters are located in the building that once served as the headquarters of historic Spooner's Ranch.

▲ Undersea sedimentary layers were compressed, lifted, tilted and eroded to create these spectacular formations.

▶ Starting a few hundred yards from the tidepools, Coon Creek Trail offers an abundance of greenery and wild flowers.

 When the waves pile the beach sand just right, fresh water runoff from Islay Creek forms this big sandy-bottom pond.

Inland from the shoreline is an ancient wave-cut terrace that was long ago uplifted from the cutting edge of the surf and now appears as a grassy coastal plain. This plain sweeps back from the ocean and then curves sharply upward to 1,500- foot-high hills that include Valencia Peak, from which one can overlook nearly 100 miles of the coastline from Point Sal in the south to Piedras Blancas in the north.

California live oak and Bishop pine grow on the chaparral covered hills, and there are willow, big leaf maple, box elder, myrtle and black cottonwood trees shade the stream-cut canyons. The park is largely undeveloped and features a wide range of birds and small wildlife. Spring and early summer re highlighted by a brilliant display of wildflowers. The predominantly yellow color of these flowers inspired the naming of this area - *Montana de Oro* or *Mountain of Gold*.

A unique feature of Montana de Oro State Park is the long sandspit that separates Morro Bay from the Ocean. It is made up of successive rows of sand dunes, some of which reach 85 feet in height. Four-wheel-drive vehicles can reach the foot of the dunes via "Dune Buggy Road," an unmarked, heavily rutted lane that runs west from Pecho Valley Road, approximately one-half mile north of the park entrance. Motor vehicles and camping are not permitted on the dunes. Within the park, motor vehicles must remain on the paved roads.

Available Activities

Your day-trip plans should be adjusted to fit current weather conditions and the physical abilities of the individuals in your group. Discuss your plans with a ranger when you arrive in case one or more of the suggested activities should be changed for your comfort and convenience.

Things to bring: sturdy walking shoes, layered clothing, swimsuit, sunscreen, insect repellant, first aid kit, towel, water, lunch, camera.

All of the suggested trails are Class 1, which means there are no irregularities higher than a standard stair step (nine inches).

This location is much too large to be fully explored in one day. The following suggested day-trip program will provide examples of several different environments:

Bluff Trail and Tide Pools: maximum 3.5 miles round trip on a smooth path along the terrace edge. 0.3 miles, including stair steps, to nearest major tide pools at Coralina Cove. Inquire at ranger station for low tide schedule, the best time to visit tidepools.

▲ Along the bluff trail nature has provided driftwood and boulders as the materials for an instant jungle gym.

▲ At low tide all of the family members can safely explore the many tidepools left on these long fingers of rock.

▲ This pitted and eroded piece of sandstone inspires exploratory touching and plenty of questions for parents.

Coon Creek Trail: 4.8 miles round trip. 300 foot elevation change. Except for several dozen steps near the trailhead, this is a smooth, easy-grade trail along a small stream in a cool, shaded canyon. Care should be taken to stay away from the abundant poison oak which is near, but not on, the path.

Spooner's Cove Beach: Parking is available adjoining this beach. Wave-carved rock formations along the main beach provide tide pools and small caves for exploration. In addition, all-year Islay Creek provides a sandy-bottom water-play area a few yards inland from the ocean waves.

▲ After a short walk from the parking area, grandparents can relax while watching the children in the pond.

▲ Over the centuries wind and water have eroded a few small caves which parents and children can explore together.

▲ The lush greenery of Coon Creek Trail is a complete change-of-pace from the open starkness of the headlands and beach.

155 MONTANA DE ORO STATE PARK

▲ This little-known part of the park is ideal for a romantic dawdle and meander.
◄ It is also ideal for surfboarding down the steep inland sides of the dunes.

Sand Spit: 1.0 miles roundtrip walk along Dune Buggy Road to reach the dunes from where you have to park a two-wheel-drive car on Pecho Valley Road. How far you choose to hike along the beach and/or the dune tops depends on your ability to walk through soft sand. Sliding down the dunes is safe and exciting fun for children of all ages.

▲ The lee-side slope of the dune is so steep that this surfer will actually coast all the way to the bottom.

▲ You don't have to have a surfboard to slide down a dune. Some exhibitionists simply roll down with reckless abandon.

Soak and Sleep

A campground with 50 spaces is available in the park. Another campground with 135 spaces and hot showers is available at nearby Morro Bay State Park. Reservations are recommended except in winter. Contact MISTIX, (800) 444-7275 from within California; (619) 452-1950 from outside California.

Embarcadero Inn: (805) 772-2700, 456 Embarcadero, Morro Bay, CA 93442. Five miles from park entrance. Offers 36 units and two hydropools.

Sycamore Hot Springs: (805) 595-7302, 1215 Avila Beach Drive, San Luis Obispo, CA 93401. Twenty miles from park entrance. Offers 26 motel units, each with a private hot tub on the balcony. Also, 35 redwood hot tubs are scattered along a hillside under the oak trees and are for rent by the hour.

◄ After a full day at the beach try a relaxing soak in a tree-shaded hot tub.

CLEVELAND NATIONAL FOREST
Trabuco Ranger District

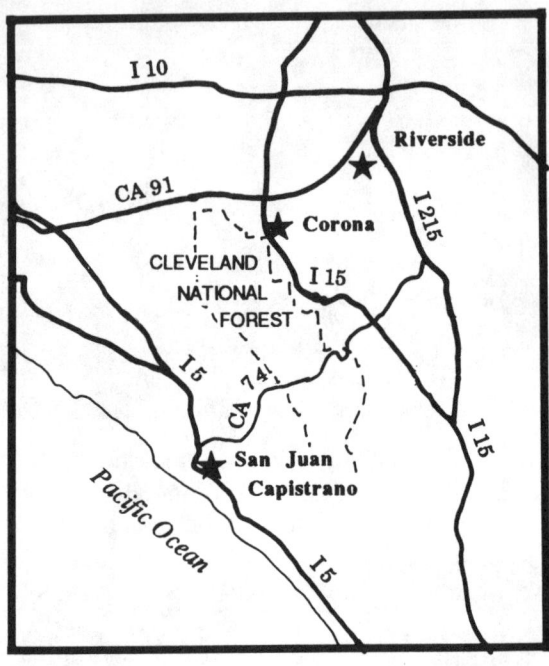

Location Overview

This Ranger District straddles the rocky Santa Ana Mountains between Lake Elsinore and San Juan Capistrano. Visits are not recommended from June to November because of excessive heat and lack of running water in the creeks. Elevation: 1,000 to 5,600 feet.

Activities include hiking and playing in seasonal streams. Equestrian and bicycle use is permitted on all trails except those in the Wilderness area. A Visitor Center near the El Cariso Campground is open on week-ends.

This Ranger District has a picnic area and five campgrounds; some spaces can be reserved through MISTIX. From the Visitor Center at El Cariso, it is five miles to motels and RV parks in Lake Elsinore; eight miles to public mineral water hot tubs at San Juan Capistrano Hot Springs; 15 miles to the Lake Elsinore Family Medical Clinic, (714) 674-6971; and 50 miles to the Ontario Airport.

▲ A recent fire killed the manzanita bush but the resilience of plant life is demonstrated by the new yucca bloom.

Tourist Attractions

Talk to your travel agent or contact the San Juan Capistrano Chamber of Commerce, 31682 El Camino Real, San Juan Capistrano, CA 92675, (714) 493-4700.

▼ The upper slopes and ridges in this location are dry and shadeless, so take along plenty of drinking water.

▲ In the wider parts of canyon bottoms oak trees provide all-year shade while every spring brings new flowers and greenery.

Trail Maps

This section identifies only a few of the activities available and does not attempt to provide detailed trail maps. Therefore, you will need an official map of the Trabuco Ranger District, Cleveland National Forest, and we recommend that you obtain it ahead of time by mail. Send your request with $2.00 to Trabuco Ranger District, 1147 E. Sixth Street, Corona, CA 91719, (714) 736-1811. Be sure to ask for supplementary information about your areas of special interest, such as natural history associations, hiking trails, camping, equestrian facilities, bicycle routes, etc.

Topography and History

A warm, dry, Mediterranean climate prevails over the Cleveland National Forest. Hot in summer but mild in winter, its elevations range from sea level to 6,000 feet. Conifers and oaks thrive in the canyons, but most of the land is exposed rocky slopes where only the hardy chaparral survives.

The Cleveland is also, by nature, a forest of fire. Annually, in the fall, hot easterly winds known as SANTA ANAS blow with gale-force intensity, causing extreme conditions that heighten the danger of fire. Historically, fires ignited during this period have consumed large acreages before they are controlled. For public safety and resource protection, OPEN FIRES IN THE CLEVELAND NATIONAL FOREST ARE PROHIBITED and fire regulations are in effect all year long.

Before European discovery, Indian tribes lived in the area near the Laguna, Palomar and Santa Ana Mountains, moving up and down the mountains with the seasons. As they began the descent to their fall encampment, hunting parties would scatter the embers of their campfires to start the annual burning. Fire was a recognized part of the natural process of regeneration because several varieties of seed-bearing pine cones would open up only after exposure to fire. Wildlife met the demands for food, skins for clothing, and feathers for ornamentation. Land and user complemented each other in a natural balance.

◄ Viewed from near the trailhead, the San Juan Loop Trail seems rather uninviting, with jagged rocks and barren slopes.

DON'T HURRY

You have permission to

dawdle & meander

See page 190

In 1769, Father Junipero Serra built the first California mission near "Old Town" in San Diego with timbers from the eastern foothills of what is now known as the Descanso Ranger District. Timbers from the Trabuco District were used to build Mission San Juan Capistrano. As new species of plants were introduced, the earlier natural balance between user and nature was altered to meet changing public needs.

In 1869, gold was discovered near Julian, attracting miners from the northern Mother Lode. During this same period, zinc, lead, and silver mines were booming in the western canyons of the Santa Ana Mountains. A large tin mine located in Trabuco Canyon was owned by Borden's Eagle Milk Company but never produced the hoped-for quantity of tin needed for the company's milk cans.

This influx of newcomers left its mark on the land. Trees were cut for shoring mine tunnels and laying ore cart trackways as well as for heat and cooking fires. Great areas of brush were burned to facilitate exploration and produce forage for livestock. The first State of California Forestry Commission, established in 1886 by Governor Stone, reflected the growing public concern for the environment.

Federal management of today's national forests began with the Creative Act of 1891, which gave the President authority to establish "Reservations" in States and Territories having public land bearing forests. In 1893 President Benjamin Harrison set the cornerstone of the Cleveland National Forest by creating the 50,000-acre Trabuco Canyon Forest Reserve in the Santa Ana Mountains. Today the total Forest covers more than 500,000 acres, managed under a multi-use policy of "the greatest good for the greatest number in the long run."

► In the bottom of the canyon, the San Juan Loop Trail becomes a delightful stroll through a shaded green meadow.

Available Activities

Your day-trip plans should be adjusted to fit current weather conditions and the physical abilities of the individuals in your group. Discuss your plans with a ranger when you arrive, in case one or more of the suggested activities should be changed for your comfort and convenience.

Things to bring: sturdy walking shoes, layered clothing, swimsuit, sunscreen, first aid kit, towel, water, lunch, camera.

Trail surfaces are classified as follows:

Class 1. Generally smooth with no irregularities larger than a standard stair step (nine inches).

Class 2. Some irregularities higher than a standard stair step, but none higher than two stair steps (18 inches).

Class 3. Some irregularities higher than 18 inches.

The location is much too large to be fully explored in one day. The following suggested day-trip program will provide examples of several different environments:

El Cariso Nature Trail Loop:

1.5 miles. 100-foot elevation change. Class 1 surface. A gentle circle route providing panoramic views of the surrounding mountains in all directions.

▲ These hikers heard a rumor that a yucca blossom had an especially sweet smell and taste. 'Twas an inflated rumor.

◄ Along the El Cariso Nature Trail Loop there is a grove of pine trees which was bypassed by the last big forest fire.

San Juan Loop Trail: 2.1 miles. 350-foot elevation change. Class 1 surface with a few Class 2 sections. Moderate grade down to and back from San Juan Creek and adjoining meadows.

▲ Rainstorms sometimes cause a trail washout, creating a temporary Class 2 section in the San Juan Loop Trail.

▲ Playing in the water feels like the right thing to do because a running stream washing sand through a bed of rocks is better than a wind up toy.

Chiquito Trail extension to San Juan Loop: 2 miles round trip. 100-foot elevation change. Class 1 surface with a few Class 2 sections. Chiquito Trail intersects with San Juan Loop Trail at San Juan Creek. Follow Chiquito Trail along the creek for one mile and then return to San Juan Trail intersection. Have lunch beside the stream.

▲ At the intersection of the San Juan Loop Trail and the Chiquito Trail, you can cross the creek without getting wet.

▼ Don't get too excited when you see gold flecks in the water; it is only iron pyrite, also known as "Fool's Gold."

Soak and Sleep

this Ranger District there are five campgrounds, me of which are closed in winter. Some spaces in e campground can be reserved through the ISTIX System, (800) 283-CAMP.

n Juan Capistrano Hot Springs: (714) 8-0400. P.O. Box 58, San Juan Capistrano, CA 693. Eight miles from the Visitor Center. mping spaces and several rental teepees are ailable. Outdoor mineral water hot tubs are for nt by the hour. Open 24 hours.

an's Motel and Mineral Spa: (714) 674- 51. 215 W. Graham, Lake Elsinore, CA 92330. ven miles from the Visitor Center. Hot mineral ter is piped to the bathtubs in all of the rooms. ere is also an indoor communal hydropool filled th 105-degree mineral water.

▲ A relaxing soak and a mutual foot rub in a tub at San Juan Capistrano Hot Springs are welcome conclusions to a full day of dawdling and meandering in nature.

◄ If all the big and little Indians in the family bring their own bedrolls they can reserve a semi-authentic teepee.(It has a board floor and a picnic table.)

MOUNT SAN JACINTO STATE PARK

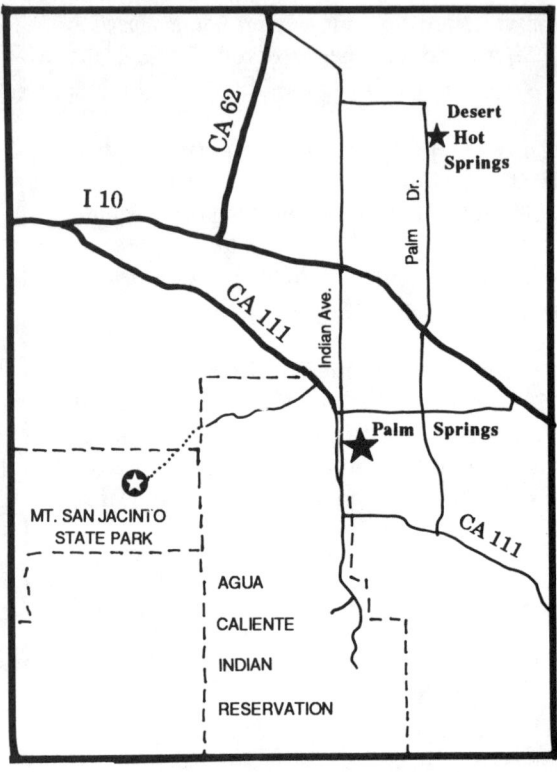

Location Overview

This 13,000-acre mountain-top wilderness state park is easily accessible via the Palm Springs Tramway. At an elevation of 8,000 feet, it is cool even in summer and some snowfall is expected from December through May.

Activities include hiking trails of various lengths and difficulties, mule train rides, and ski lessons in winter. No motorcycles, bicycles or dogs are permitted. There is a Visitor Center in the Tram Mountain Station and a Ranger Station at the Wilderness area trailhead.

There are no overnight accommodations at either end of the Tram, and there is no overnight parking in the Tram parking lot. Commercial campsites, RV spaces and hotel rooms are available three miles away in Palm Springs and ten miles north in Desert Hot Springs. Day-use mineral water hot pools are available in Desert Hot Springs until 10 pm. It is five miles to Desert Hospital, (619) 323-6511, and four miles to the Palm Springs Airport.

▲ The eastern edge of this mountain-top location overlooks miles of desert, and a few cities, in the Coachella Valley.

▲ This couple, and their families, came all the way from the Midwest to get married in this beautiful park.

Tourist Attractions

Talk to your travel agent or contact the Palm Springs Chamber of Commerce, 190 W. Amado Road, Palm Springs, CA 92262, (619) 325-1577.

Trail Maps

This section identifies only a few of the activities available and does not attempt to provide a detailed trail map. Therefore, you will need an official map of the Mount San Jacinto State Park, and we recommend that you obtain it ahead of time by mail. Send your request with $1.00 to Mount San Jacinto State Wilderness, P.O. Box 308, Idyllwild, CA 92549, (714) 659-2607. Be sure to ask for supplementary information about your areas of special interest, such as local natural history associations, guided nature walks, camping, hiking trails, equestrian facilities, bicycle routes, etc.

Topography and History

The deeply weathered summit of Mount San Jacinto stands 10,804 feet above sea level, the highest point in the San Jacinto Range and the second highest in Southern California. No more than a two-hour drive from either Los Angeles or San Diego, the mountain's magnificent granite peaks, subalpine forests, and fern-bordered mountain meadows offer a unique opportunity to explore and enjoy a scenic high-country wilderness.

▲ This tram ride is an exciting part of the trip, but is only the beginning.

The upper slopes of the mountain have changed little since early man roamed its meadows and forests in search of game. For the Cahuilla Indians, this was a sacred place - the home of Dakush, the legendary founder of the Cahuilla people, and Tahquitz, an evil and powerful demon with an insatiable appetite for human flesh. For the Cahuilla, thunder and lightning above the mountain meant that Tahquitz was angry.

Starting in Chino Canyon, the Palm Springs Tramway takes passengers from the Valley Station at 2,643 feet elevation to Mountain Station on the edge of the Wilderness, at 8,516 feet. It took two years and thousands of helicopter flights to build the two stations and four steel towers that support cables more than two miles long. Two 80-passenger cars travel in alternate directions as they cover a vertical distance of 5,873 feet in 14 minutes. The Mountain Station features a restaurant, gift shop, snack bar and the State Park Visitor Center. The Tram operates year-around except for a maintenance closure in August. For more information about hours of operation and time schedules, call the Palm Springs Aerial Tramway at (619) 325-1391.

In Long Valley, a short walk from the station, you will find a picnic area with stoves and restrooms, a ski center, a self-guiding nature trail, and the Desert View Trail, which offers panoramas of the high country, including several peaks over 10,000 feet in elevation. You will also find the Long Valley Ranger Station, which controls entry into the Wilderness trail system.

You must obtain a permit before entering the Wilderness. These permits are free; they limit the number of hikers to assure solitude and to protect the wilderness resource from overuse. The growing season is short in the San Jacinto high country, and plant life has little opportunity to recover from heavy use during the summer months. The permit system has been established to preserve the wild beauty of the back country by keeping use within the carrying capacity of the Wilderness. Day-use permits can be obtained on the day of your visit at the Long Valley Ranger Station.

▲ At the Tram Mountain Station, there is a buffet restaurant with some outdoor tables on a patio overlooking the tram.

▼ Mountain Station also includes a visitor center, a gift shop, and this patio overlooking the forest in the park.

169 MT. SAN JACINTO STATE PARK

▲ Wilderness permits are not required for these two well-marked trails, that are the nearest to Mountain Station.

▲ This gracious sign is mounted on the deck at the Ranger Station where wilderness permits are issued for hiking to any of the other trails in the area.

Available Activities

Your day-trip plans should be adjusted to fit current weather conditions and the physical abilities of the individuals in your group. Discuss your plans with a ranger when you arrive, in case one or more of the suggested activities should be changed for your comfort and convenience.

Things to bring: sturdy walking shoes, layered clothing, sunscreen, insect repellant, first aid kit, towel, water, lunch, camera.

Trail surfaces are classified as follows:

Class 1. Generally smooth with no irregularities higher than a standard stair step (nine inches).

Class 2. Some irregularities higher than a standard stair step, but none larger than two stair steps (18 inches).

Class 3. Some irregularities higher than 18 inches.

This location is much too large to be fully explored in one day. The following suggested day-trip program will provide examples of several different environments:

▲ For those willing to hike through some steep sections, Desert View Trail does deliver a spectacular desert view.

▼ For those who prefer to ride with a guide, this mule train at least takes you well out into the woods.

Desert View Trail: 1.5 miles. 800-foot elevation change. Class 1 surface with some Class 2 sections. Beautiful, sometimes-steep trail leading to a spectacular view of the Coachella Valley and surrounding mountains.

Nature Loop Trail: 0.6 miles. Minor elevation change. Class 1 surface. Printed guide booklets are available at the trailhead. Note: The available mule train ride follows a similar route through this area.

Round Valley Loop Trail: 4.1 miles. 1,000-foot elevation change. Class 1 surface with some Class 2 sections. This route follows an uneven but well-marked trail along Long Valley Creek and returns via Round Valley.

▲
◆
▼ Along the trail, snow bridges over the creek invite exploration and quiet forest vistas invite contemplation.

▲ When the snow melts in the spring, larger and larger portions of the Round Valley Loop Trail become usable.

Soak and Sleep

There are no overnight accommodations at either end of the Tram, and there is no overnight parking in the Tram parking lot.

Palm Springs Spa Hotel: (619)325-1461. 100 N. Indian Avenue, Palm Springs, CA 92262. Three miles from the Tram entrance. Rooms and a complete spa, with multiple mineral-water pools available to the public. Call for hours.

Las Palmas Equestrian/RV Park: (619) 322-0031. 3787 Sonora Road, Palm Springs, CA 92262. Five miles from the Tram entrance. Commercial campsites, RV spaces and equestrian care are available.

Desert Hot Springs Spa and Hotel: (619) 329-6495. 10805 Palm Drive, Desert Hot Springs, CA 92240. Ten miles from the Tram entrance. The central courtyard includes many large, mineral-water soaking pools maintained at various temperatures. Day use available until 10 pm. Massage available by appointment.

 At the Palm Springs Spa Hotel you have a choice of a shaded soaking pool or a sunny swimming pool with recliners.

INDIAN CANYONS

Tourist Attractions

Talk to your travel agent or contact Palm Springs Chamber of Commerce, 190 W. Amado Road, Palm Springs, CA 92262, (619) 325-1577.

▲ Sparkling streams of melted snow from the nearby mountain nourish the lush greenery in otherwise barren canyons.

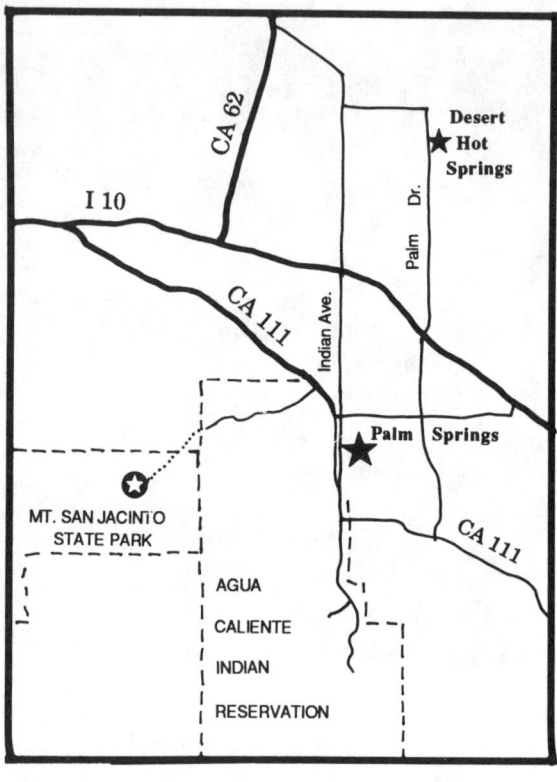

Location Overview

The Cahuilla Indian Reservation covers 32,000 acres on the east flank of Mt. San Jacinto and the nearby desert slopes. The reservation includes four spectacular palm-filled canyons, carved and watered by the runoff from Mt. San Jacinto. Elevation: 1,000 to 2,000 feet. Open 8 am to 5 pm. Closed July and August.

The activities include exploring the canyons and playing in the streams. Equestrian stables in Palm Springs also offer group rides into portions of the canyons.

There are no accommodations in the canyons, and overnight parking is not permitted in the parking lots. Commercial campsites, RV spaces, hotel rooms, and day-use, mineral-water hot pools are available in Palm Springs and also ten miles north in Desert Hot Springs. It is four miles to Desert Hospital, (619) 323-6511, and three miles to the Palm Springs Airport.

Visitors to the canyons are dwarfed by the tall palm trees and spectacular formations of carved volcanic rock.

Trail Maps

This section does not attempt to provide a detailed trail map. Therefore, you will need an official map of the Indian Canyons, and we recommend that you obtain it ahead of time by mail. Send your request to Tribal Council Office, 960 E. Taquitz Canyon Way, Suite 106, Palm Springs, CA 92262, (619) 325-5673. Be sure to ask for supplementary information about your areas of special interest, such as local natural history associations, guided nature walks, hiking trails, equestrian facilities, bicycle routes, etc.

▲ Nature finds a thousand different ways to arrange rocks, palm trees and running water within a canyon 15 miles long.

Topography and History

Centuries ago, ancestors of the AG[UA] CALIENTE CAHUILLA (pronounced Kaw-we-[ya]) INDIANS settled in the Palm Springs area a[nd] developed extensive and complex communitie[s in] Palm, Murray, Andreas, Tahquitz and Ch[ino] Canyons. Abundant water and hundreds of pla[nts] and animals found throughout the area ensu[red] stable living conditions. Crops of melons, squa[sh,] beans and corn were grown, animals were hun[ted] and plants and seeds were gathered for fo[od,] medicines, basket weaving, etc. Many traces [of] these communities exist in the canyons tod[ay,] including rock art, house pits and foundatio[ns,] irrigation ditches, dams, reservoirs, trails and f[ood] processing areas.

The AGUA CALIENTE INDIANS w[ere] industrious and creative, with a reputation [for] independence, integrity and peace. They belie[ved] this productive land of their ancestors would alw[ays] be theirs, but in 1876 the U.S. Federal Governm[ent] deeded to them in trust 32,000 acres to be used [as] their homeland. At the same time the governm[ent] gave to the Southern Pacific Railroad ten miles [of] the odd-numbered sections of land on either side [of] the railroad right of way. Of the reservatio[n's] 32,000 acres, some 6,700 lie within the P[alm] Springs city limits. The remaining even-numbe[red] sections fan out across the desert and mountain[s in] a checkerboard pattern.

Fifteen miles long, Palm Canyon is one of [the] great places of beauty in western North Ameri[ca.] Its indigenous flora and fauna, which [the] CAHUILLA people so expertly used, and [its] abundant Washingtonia filifera (palm trees) [are] breathtaking contrasts to the stark rocky gorges a[nd] barren desert lands beyond. From the Trading P[ost] a moderately graded, paved footpath winds do[wn] into the canyon for picnicking near the stre[am,] meditating, exploring, hiking or horseback ridin[g.]

▲ Barren rocks and desert sand are typical of the area except where canyon palm trees trace the paths of running water.

The lush oasis of Andreas Canyon offers the contrasting greens of magnificent fan palms and more than 150 species of plants within a half-mile radius. A boulder-strewn footpath winds through the canyon, passing groves of skirted palms and unusual rock formations (some containing CAHUILLA rock art). Along all-year Andreas Creek it is still possible to see the bedrock mortars and metates used centuries ago for preparing food.

Murray Canyon is reached via a quarter-mile hike across barren land from the Andreas Canyon parking area. Good foot and equestrian trails lead to beautiful recreational spots among the many palm trees. Peninsula Big Horn Sheep (an endangered species), wild ponies and other wild animals still roam the high ground above the canyon. Being less visited, Murray Canyon has its own secluded beauty.

Tahquitz Canyon, just west of the city of Palm Springs, is noted for its magnificent waterfalls and pools. Evidence suggests that it supported a large population of CAHUILLA INDIANS. Abundant wildlife and plant life are present throughout. Planning is under way to establish the Agua Caliente Cultural Museum here in the near future. Tahquitz Canyon is closed to the public until further notice.

▲ Picnic tables have been installed in shady palm groves at the lower end of Palm Canyon and Andreas Canyon.

▶ ▼ Weather-carved volcanic rock walls provide a stark contrast to green palms. Palm Canyon is a verdant gash through acres of twisted lava formations.

Available Activities

Your day-trip plans should be adjusted to fit current weather conditions and the physical abilities of the individuals in your group. Discuss your plans with the gate attendant when you arrive, in case one or more of the activities should be changed for your comfort and convenience.

Things to bring: sturdy walking shoes, layered clothing, swimsuit, sunscreen, insect repellant, first aid kit, towel, water, lunch, camera.

Trail surfaces are classified as follows:
Class 1. Generally smooth with no irregularities higher than a standard stair step (nine inches).
Class 2. Some irregularities higher than a standard stair step but none higher than two stair steps (18 inches).
Class 3. Some irregularities higher than 18 inches.

It is not practical to fully explore any one of three accessible canyons in a single day. The following suggested day-trip program will provide examples of different environments:

Palm Canyon: Your hike extends as far as you choose to go, allowing for your return trip before closing time. The elevation gain is very gentle, and a Class 1 foot path winds through the palms in the wide lower canyon. For each mile you go upstream, the rock formations become more spectacular and the trail surface adds a few more Class 2 spots.

Andreas Canyon: This trail requires quite a bit of Class 3 boulder-hopping, so the length of your round trip hike will be limited by your agility and stamina and by the 5 pm closing time. The overall elevation change of the stream is moderate, but the trail route has a few strenuous spots. However, the spectacular beauty is worth quite a bit of bother.

▲ These Andreas Canyon visitors are following the trail along the stream. Boulder-hopping like this starts within 100 yards of the parking area.

▲ In some places it is easier to walk in the stream than scramble on the trail.

◄ Near the parking area, this small dam holds a delightful shallow splash pool.

▲
▶ Very few visitors hike to the upper reaches of Murray Canyon, so skinnydippers enjoy splashing and tannning without offending anyone.

Alternate Day-Trip Program:

Murray Canyon: Because of its distance fro[m] parking area, this beautiful canyon draws far fe[wer] visitors than the other two. Hike as far as you l[ike] but allow time for your return trip before [the] closing hour. A gentle elevation gain with a C[lass] 1 surface in the lower reaches gradually beco[mes] Class 2 and 3 as you go farther upstream.

Soak and Sleep

There are no overnight accommodations in the Indian Canyons, and overnight parking is not permitted anywhere on the property.

Palm Springs Spa Hotel: (619)325-1461. 100 N. Indian Avenue, Palm Springs, CA 92262. Three miles from the Tram entrance. Rooms and a complete spa with multiple mineral-water pools are available to the public.

Las Palmas Equestrian/RV Park: (619) 322-0031. 3787 Sonora Road, Palm Springs, CA 92262. Five miles from the Tram entrance. Commercial campsites, RV spaces, and equestrian care are available.

Desert Hot Springs Spa and Hotel: (619) 329-6495. 10805 Palm Drive, Desert Hot Springs, CA 92240. Ten miles from the Tram entrance. The central courtyard includes many large, mineral-water soaking pools maintained at various temperatures. Day use available until 10 pm. Massage available by appointment.

The Palm Springs Spa Hotel is built on Indian land which is also the hot spring source for the mineral water used in the outdoor pools and bathhouse tubs.

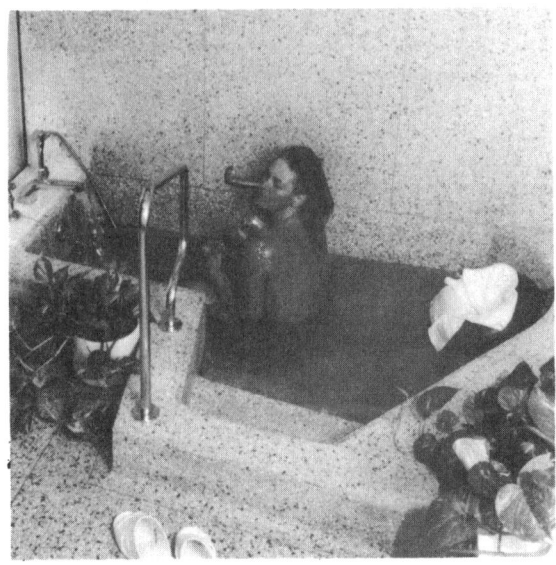

JOSHUA TREE NATIONAL MONUMENT

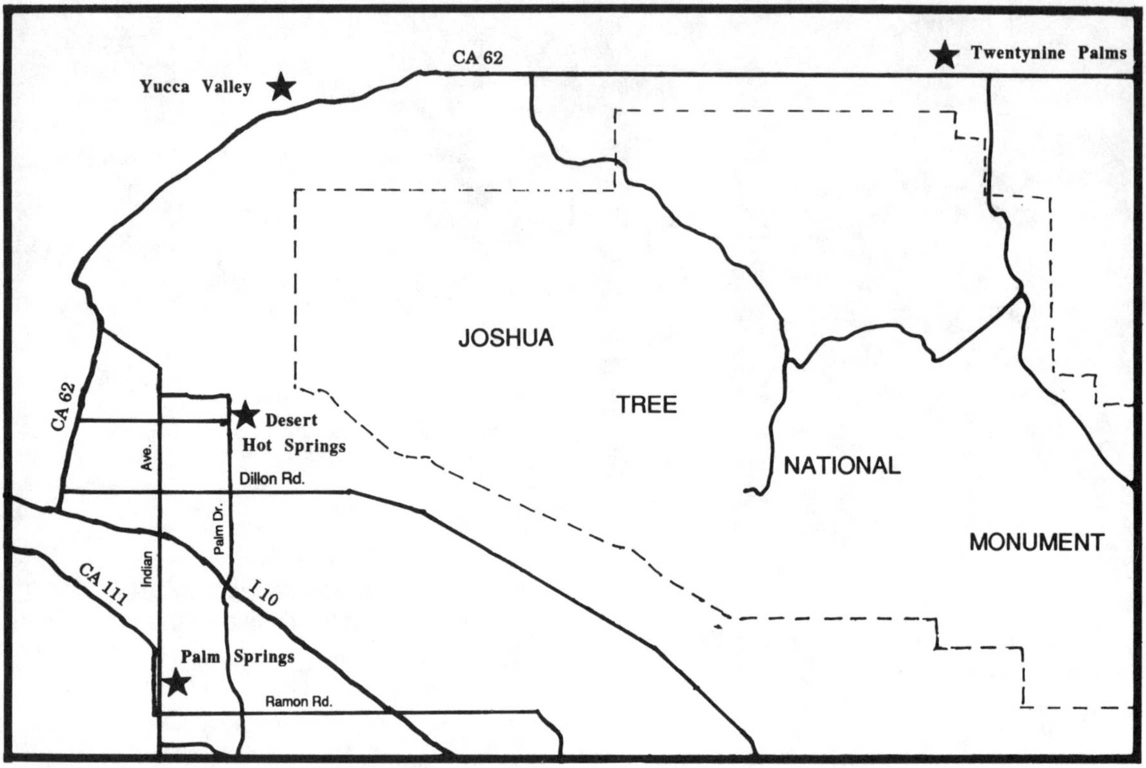

Location Overview

The monument covers more than a half-million acres, including both high desert and low desert topography. Be prepared for high temperatures in July and August; carry plenty of water. Elevation: 2,500 to 4,500 feet.

There is a wide range of opportunities for activity, including two Visitor Centers, short self-guided nature trails (two of which are wheelchair accessible), longer trails, dedicated equestrian trails, and some opportunities for mountain biking.

Nine campgrounds are available within the monument, and a few of the spaces can be reserved through the Ticketron reservation system. Measured from the West Entrance, it is ten miles to motels and RV parks; 25 miles to day-use mineral-water hot pools; 20 miles to High Desert Hospital, (619) 365-7635; and 45 miles to the Palm Springs Airport.

Tourist Attractions

Talk to your travel agent or contact Palm Springs Chamber of Commerce, 190 W. Amado Road, Palm Springs, CA 92262, (619) 325-1577.

Trail Maps

This section identifies only a few of the activities available and does not attempt to provide a detailed trail map. Therefore, you will need an official map of Joshua Tree National Monument, and we recommend that you obtain it ahead of time by mail. To request a park brochure, write to Superintendent, Joshua Tree National Monument, 74485 National Monument Drive, Twentynine Palms, CA 92277. Be sure to ask for supplementary information about your areas of special interest, such as local natural history associations, guided nature walks, camping, hiking trails, equestrian facilities, bicycle routes, etc. Detailed trail maps are available for sale at the park visitor centers.

▲ Barren hills and Joshua trees extend for miles in a natural desert setting unmarred by off-road vehicle tracks or other souvenirs of civilization.

▲ The monument, containing much more than sand and cactus, includes miles of these spectacular rock formations.

183 JOSHUA TREE NATIONAL MONUMENT

▲ Some of the landscape looks like a huge jungle gym built of rocks, inviting every passerby to come and climb for a while.

▲ Miles of designated gravel roads are smooth enough for use by standard bicycles as well as by mountain bikes.

Topography and History

The desert is immense and infinitely variable, yet delicately fragile. It is land shaped by sudden torrents of rain and climatic extremes. Rainfall is sparse and unpredictable. Streambeds are usually dry and waterholes are few. This land may appear defeated and dead, but within its parched environment are intricate living systems, each fragment performing a slightly different function, and each depending upon the whole system for survival.

Two deserts, their large ecosystems primarily determined by elevation, come together at Joshua Tree National Monument. Few areas more vividly illustrate the contrast between high and low desert. Below 3,000 feet, the Colorado Desert, which occupies the eastern half of the monument, is dominated by the abundant creosotebush. The higher, slightly cooler and wetter Mohave Desert is the special habitat of the undisciplined Joshua Tree.

Standing like islands in a desolate sea, the oases, a third ecosystem, provide dramatic contrast to their arid surroundings. Five fan-palm oases dot the monument, indicating those few areas where water occurs naturally at or near the surface and meets the special life requirements of these stately trees.

The monument encompasses some of the most interesting geologic displays found in California deserts. Rugged mountains of twisted rock and exposed granite monoliths testify to the tremendous earth forces that shaped and formed this land. Arroyos, playas, alluvial fans, bajadas, pediments, desert varnish, granites, aplite and gneiss interact to form a giant desert mosaic of immense beauty and complexity.

As old as the desert may look, it is but a temporary phenomenon in the time-scale of geology. In more verdant times, one of the Southwest's earliest inhabitants, Pinto Man, lived here, hunting and gathering along a slow moving river that ran through now dry Pinto Basin. Later, Indians traveled through this area in tune with the harvests of pinyon nuts, mesquite beans, acorns and cactus fruit, leaving behind rock paintings and pottery ollas as reminders of their passing.

In the late 1800s, explorers, cattlemen and miners came to the desert. They built dams to create water tanks and dug up and tunneled the earth in search of gold. They are gone now, and left behind are their remnants, the Lost Horse and Desert Queen Mines and the Desert Queen Ranch. In the 1930s, homesteaders came seeking free land and the chance to start new lives. Today many people come to the monument seeking clear skies, clean air, and the peace and tranquility, quietude and beauty that only deserts offer.

▲ Very few campsites offer any shade, but the more interesting campgrounds are surrounded by graceful rock formations.

▲ Experienced rock climbers can often be seen practicing their skills on the more difficult vertical rock faces.

▲ During windless early morning hours the surface of Barker Dam Reservoir is mirror smooth, vividly reflecting the green trees, brown rocks, and blue sky.

▲ To help keep the area in its beautiful natural state, dogs, fires, camping, bicycles, and swimming are prohibited.

Available Activities

Your day-trip plans should be adjusted to fit current weather conditions and the physical abilities of the individuals in your group. Discuss your plans with a ranger when you arrive, in case one or more of the suggested activities should be changed for your comfort and convenience.

Things to bring: sturdy walking shoes, layered clothing, sunscreen, insect repellant, first aid kit, water, lunch, camera.

Trail surfaces are classified as follows:

Class 1. Generally smooth with no irregularities higher than a standard stair step (nine inches).

Class 2. Some irregularities higher than a standard stair step, but none higher than two stair steps (18 inches).

Class 3. Some irregularities higher than 18 inches.

This location is much too large to be explored in one day. The following suggested day-trip program will provide examples of several different environments:

Barker Dam and Reservoir: 1.1 miles round trip. Minor elevation change. Mostly smooth Class 1 surface with some Class 2 and Class 3 sections near the dam. Site includes Indian campsites and petroglyphs.

Hidden Valley Nature Trail Loop: 1.1 miles. Less than 100-foot elevation change. Class 1 surface with some Class 2 sections. Trailside signs interpret the plant life and cattle rustling history of this area.

Although near a convenient parking area, Hidden Valley is serenely quiet, fully shielded from the sounds of vehicles.

187 JOSHUA TREE NATIONAL MONUMENT

▲ Some campers choose to sleep out under the stars and be greeted with this classic desert scene when dawn arrives.

▼ Early morning temperatures in the high desert call for layered clothing, that can be peeled off as the sun rises.

Skull Rock Nature Trail Loop: 1.7 mile from start in Jumbo Rocks Campground. Less tha 100-foot elevation change. Class 1 surface wi some Class 2 sections. Trailside signs explain th spectacular environment.

Soak and Sleep

Black Canyon Campground, in Joshua Tree National Monument, has spaces that may be reserved through the Ticketron reservation system, (800) 452-1111. All of the other eight monument campgrounds operate on a first-come, first-served basis.

Desert Hot Springs Spa and Motel: (619) 329-6495. 10805 Palm Drive, Desert Hot Springs, CA 92240. Twenty two miles from the West Entrance. The central courtyard includes many large, mineral-water soaking pools maintained at various temperatures. Day use is available until 10 pm. Massage available by appointment.

Sam's Family Spa: (619) 329-6457. 70875 Dillon Road, Desert Hot Springs, CA 92240. Twenty seven miles from West Entrance. A 40-acre RV park that also offers some rooms with kitchenette suites. The semi-enclosed pool building contains four large, chlorine-free mineral water soaking pools maintained at various temperatures. Day use is available until 7 pm.

29 Palms RV Resort: (619) 367-3320. 4949 Desert Knoll Avenue, Twentynine Palms, CA 92777. This resort offers a golf course and tennis courts in addition to a tap-water hot pool.

▲ This multi-pool courtyard at Desert Hot Springs Spa and Motel adjoins a bar, restaurant, health club and gift shop.

▲ Some campers reserve a space in Black Canyon Campground and then, after arriving, go look for a better space in the first-come/first-served campgrounds, such as Jumbo Rocks Campground.

THE ULTIMATE STRESS-REDUCTION MESSAGE

DON'T RUSH ME
I have permission to

DON'T HURRY
You have permission to

For a free catalog of our T shirts, publications and products, send your name and address to
CATALOG, 55 Azalea Lane, Santa Cruz, CA 95060

DAY TRIPS in CALIFORNIA Nature

Jayson Loam
Luis Gonzalez
Karen Cunningham

with nearby hot pools, campgrounds, and accommodations

This unique guidebook is designed for independent people who want to enjoy a single-day stroll through natural surroundings, without sweaty backpacks or noisy tour buses, and then savor a relaxing soak in a hot pool. Hundreds of photos illustrate 22 prime locations. Available nonstrenuous activities, some suitable for seniors, families or the handicapped, are described in detail, including opportunities to just dawdle and meander, or walk on logs, climb on rocks and play in running streams.

Buy at any bookstore
or order by mail:
Send $14.95
+ $2.00 shipping to
DAY TRIPS
55 Azalea Lane
Santa Cruz, CA 95060

Jayson Loam's guidebooks are the definitive sources for places where you can legally put your body in hot water.

- COLORADO
- UTAH
- NEVADA
- CALIFORNIA
- BAJA(MEXICO)
- ARIZONA
- NEW MEXICO
- TEXAS

Hot Springs and Hot Pools of the Southwest

ISBN# 0-9624830-1-X
Publication: March 1991

- ALASKA
- ALBERTA
- BRITISH COLUMBIA
- WASHINGTON
- OREGON
- IDAHO
- MONTANA
- WYOMING

Hot Springs and Hot Pools of the Northwest

ISBN# 0-9624830-2-8
Publication: March 1992

His user-friendly format provides a complete description and a specific key map location for every spring listed.

Dozens of easy-to-read maps and hundreds of photos help you make an informed choice, tell you how to get there, and show you what to expect when you arrive. 160 pages, 8 1/2" by 11".

Descriptions of free-flowing primitive hot springs include information about the general environment, the elevation, the types of volunteer-built soaking pools, the bathing suit customs, and the distance to campgrounds and other services. Descriptions of commercial geothermal establishments include information about the surroundings, pool sizes, water temperatures and chemical water treatment, plus available bathhouse health and beauty programs. Recreation facilities and related services offered on the premises are also listed.

In addition to natural hot spring locations, these comprehensive guides include drilled geothermal wells and urban rent-a-tub locations which offer gas-heated tap-water hot pools in private spaces for rent by the hour.

ORDER BY MAIL

Send $14.95 + $2.00 shipping to
A.T.A. Southwest
55 Azalea Lane Santa Cruz, CA 95060

ORDER BY MAIL

Send $14.95 + $2.00 shipping to
A.T.A. Northwest
55 Azalea Lane Santa Cruz, CA 95060